THE BASICS

of

LEADING

a

CHILD-CARE BUSINESS

THE BUSINESS OF CHILD CARE

Marnie Forestieri

Gryphon House

COPYRIGHT

© 2021 Marnie Forestieri

Published by Gryphon House, Inc.
P. O. Box 10, Lewisville, NC 27023
800.638.0928; 877.638.7576 [fax]

Visit us on the web at www.gryphonhouse.com.

All rights reserved. No part of this publication may be reproduced
or transmitted in any form or by any means, electronic or technical,
including photocopy, recording, or any information storage or retrieval
system, without prior written permission of the publisher. Printed in
the United States. Every effort has been made to locate copyright and
permission information.

LIBRARY OF CONGRESS CONTROL NUMBER:
2020948126.

BULK PURCHASE

Gryphon House books are available for special premiums and
sales promotions as well as for fund-raising use. Special editions or
book excerpts also can be created to specifications. For details, call
800.638.0928.

DISCLAIMER

Gryphon House, Inc., cannot be held responsible for damage, mishap,
or injury incurred during the use of or because of activities in this book.
Appropriate and reasonable caution and adult supervision of children
involved in activities and corresponding to the age and capability of
each child involved are recommended at all times. Do not leave children
unattended at any time. Observe safety and caution at all times.

This book is not intended to give legal or financial advice. All financial
and legal opinions contained herein are from the personal research and
experience of the author and are intended as educational material. Seek
the advice of a qualified legal advisor or financial advisor before making
legal or financial decisions.

CONTENTS

INTRODUCTION

Leading a child-care center and developing a quality workforce is a huge challenge. The landscape of the child-care industry has changed dramatically over the past several years, making those challenges even more difficult. Child-care operators and providers are rethinking how they can provide high-quality care for young children. Families are rethinking whether the cost of child care is necessary.

America's decentralized early childhood system ranges from small in-home day-care centers to larger child-care centers supported by families' fees and/or public subsidies. According to the *Early Childhood Workforce Index—2018*, approximately one million adults employed at center-based programs cared for and educated millions of children from birth to the age of five years. Another one million child-care professionals worked in informal settings. These caregivers are an ethnically, linguistically, and racially diverse—as well as predominately female—workforce.

The American child-care system supports the country's economy. Businesses rely on employees. Employees rely on child care. Working families face the same challenges as the generations that preceded them: how to provide care for their young children while they are away at work.

In her 2016 article "Is the Cost of Childcare Driving Women Out of the U.S. Workforce?" Bridget Ansel asserts that the lack of family-friendly policies to support women in the workforce explains the decrease in women's participation in recent years. In contrast, European countries with expanded policies such as family leave, child-care subsidies, and part-time work encourage women's employment. As more families rely on dual incomes to stay afloat, women's long-term financial well-being is at risk, especially in the case of divorce or a partner's death.

A 2018 survey conducted by the Center for American Progress reflected that mothers were 40 percent more likely than fathers to report that they had personally felt the negative impact of child-care issues on their career and said they would take steps to increase their earnings and advance their careers if child care was available (Halpin, Agne, and Omero, 2018).

According to researcher Sandra Bishop-Josef and her colleagues in 2019, the cost of lost earnings, productivity, and revenue due to the child-care crisis totals an estimated $57 billion.

Lack of access to high-quality, affordable child care continues to drive parents out of the workforce, disproportionately impacting women's careers. The trend especially affects minority women. Bishop-Josef and colleagues found that minority women reported that they would look for higher-paying jobs if they had better access to child care.

Child-care businesses rely on family tuition to support their businesses. In a landscape plagued by income inequality, child-care operators who are making a reasonable profit are the ones serving the high-to-middle-income family bracket in areas where families can afford to pay higher tuition rates. The rest operate at very thin margins.

Regardless of the profitability, labor remains the leading operational risk child-care centers face across all market segments. To hire, retain, and develop a trained and stable workforce, businesses have to create the salaries, conditions, career paths, culture, and processes for professionals to enter and remain in the industry. All components of the child-care system have to work together to shape the image of the child-care professional of the twenty-first century.

By 2020, a new child-care landscape had started taking shape. The COVID-19 pandemic exposed the vulnerabilities of the system and highlighted the importance of early childhood education as a pillar of the economy. Essential workers struggled to find child care so they could continue to keep their jobs. The pandemic emphasized the longstanding struggles of working families to access high-quality, affordable child-care solutions. It also brought to light the challenges of private child-care businesses operating on thin margins and in less-than-ideal conditions.

With these challenges come opportunities. We have learned about the importance of teacher-child interactions in setting the foundation for children's success in school and understand that child-care professionals play a key role. While the COVID-19 crisis forced some child-care centers to close permanently and reduced the child-care workforce, it also started a national conversation about the opportunity to reshape the post-pandemic child-care landscape in America and the importance of involving the federal government in setting the respect, conditions, and environment that would allow families to access affordable, high-quality child-care.

Bishop-Josef and colleagues point out that policies such as the Child Care and Development Block Grant (CCDBG) of 2014 and the Child Care for Working Families Act of 2019 represent great progress in crafting solutions to increase access to child care and support families. The National Association for the Education of Young Children (NAEYC) and other organizations are leading conversations to propose solutions to elevate the careers of child-care professionals after COVID-19. Our nation has the opportunity to work together to find solutions on how to attract, hire, and retain the next generation of child-care professionals.

THE RAPID SPEED OF CHANGE

With a solid foundation, child-care centers can adapt to changing conditions and withstand uncertainty. The convergence of uncertainty, complexity, and acceleration demands a response that ignites passion and meaning and purpose in the workforce, asserts Ira Wolfe in his book *Recruiting in the Age of Googlization*; I agree, especially after COVID-19. To rebuild our shattered child-care landscape, owners and directors will have to adapt their approach to leading child-care organizations.

As changes unfold in front of our eyes, the presumption that employers will offer long-term jobs may be a thing of the past. Free agency and the gig economy (the economy of freelance and part-time workers) in the new generations, along with the uncertainties imposed by our post-pandemic world, will require a certain comfort with sharing the workplace. Organizations will require leadership, speed, flexibility, analysis, and technology.

In his book *The Age of Spiritual Machines: When Computers Exceed Human Intelligence*, Ray Kurzweil explains, "We are entering the age of acceleration. Because of exponential growth, the 21st century will be equivalent to 20,000 years of programs at today's rate of progress and will require organizations to adapt at a faster and faster pace. Therefore, there will be only one constant element in the organizations of the 21st century: change."

A Chinese proverb says that "when the winds of change blow, some build walls and others build windmills." Change will require employers to build windmills as they adapt and differentiate their child-care centers. Offering a strong, flexible, respectful, and supportive culture in your child-care center will become the differentiator to creating a stable workforce.

DEVELOPING THIS SERIES

This book is the second in the Basics of Child Care series on starting and operating a child-care business. To provide information relevant to child-care operators and to directors who want to understand the management side of the operations, we sent out a needs-assessment survey to providers serving different market segments. One of the survey findings is that, regardless of the organizational structure or business model, all child-care providers face the same challenges: operations, marketing, finances, and customer service.

In most cases, directors who responded to our survey say they report to an owner who handles the business side of the operation. One of the challenges of this dual-management system model—an investor/owner and a child-care director—is that it prevents directors from having a holistic view of the company. The high costs of setting up a program and lack of understanding of the business side of the industry, financing options, and challenges of opening a new business have kept educators from understanding the total picture. Owners handle the business side of the operation, including selecting a location, marketing the facility, securing financing, setting and processing payroll, collecting money, and paying business expenses. Educators manage staff, provide customer service, and are accountable for quality metrics of the program.

Nevertheless, directors know from experience that decisions made in one area of the company will affect the rest of the organization. Child-care directors who understand the business side of the operation can operate more efficiently and respond faster to market trends, as the organizations of the twenty-first century will demand that internal departments be interconnected. In the same way, child-care owners who understand the skills, knowledge, and techniques needed to support children's development and learning can design and support high-quality programs with their administrative decisions. As states develop guidelines to cover skills and knowledge children are expected to learn, both sides of the business of child care must work together to meet the expectations of what children should learn before entering formal school. This book is designed to create a shared vision for both sides of the operation.

HOW THIS BOOK IS ORGANIZED

Each chapter focuses on a specific area of operations, offering terminology and concepts to help you understand the ins and outs of the child-care business. You will find the following features throughout the book:

- **Terms to Know:** vocabulary related to the key concepts

- **Main Questions:** key questions that shape each chapter

- **Case Study:** real-life or fictional scenarios that illustrate key concepts

- **Build Your Knowledge:** questions and exercises to help you apply the concepts you are learning

I share case studies of providers in different settings, including home care, independent day care, and franchised locations. At the end of each chapter, you can build your knowledge with guided questions that will help you assess your progress.

DEVELOPING AND LEADING A HIGH-QUALITY PROGRAM

Before you begin this journey, take stock of the key components of a high-quality child-care program. High-quality programs are easy to spot. From the moment you enter the facility, you can experience children's joy for learning, recognize intentional and caring teachers, explore carefully designed spaces, and observe health and safety practices.

All states have regulations or licensing standards that child-care providers must meet to legally operate in the state. The regulations provide a baseline of quality rather than one advancing child development and early learning. Different tools have been developed to compare and measure excellence, such as environmental rating scales, the Quality Rating and Improvement System (QRIS), and national accreditations. Quality-improvement systems such as accreditations evaluate a program's commitment to high-quality standards by looking at teacher-child, teacher-family, and community relationships, as well as leadership and management.

Regardless of the tools, there are some key components of quality to measure and compare the quality of early learning.

- **Environment:** High-quality programs offer children a physical setting where they can play, explore, and learn safely. Staff follow procedures for diapering, sanitizing, and food services.

- **Program structure:** The leadership supports developmentally appropriate practices, balanced learning, quality-improvement processes, and a pipeline of well-trained teachers.

- **Curriculum:** The written plan detailing the activities and experiences to support children's learning is age appropriate, grounded in child-development principles, and evidence based; provides ongoing assessments; and supports family involvement and individualized instruction.

- **Supportive interactions:** Adults respond quickly to children's needs, respect their opinions, and help them self-regulate.

What all these components have in common is that they require a well-educated, committed, and trained workforce. We will look at the barriers to hiring such a workforce and explore ways to get around these barriers, exploring solutions designed around the motivations and ideal profile of the candidates. Motivation has long been recognized as an important factor in the quality of a person's work in any vocation, and that is especially accurate in a vocation such as teaching early learners.

Growing into a high-quality program begins with a commitment to excellence at all times. Going through the process will not be easy; it may be the hardest thing you have ever done. It will require every member of the school family to be involved. You will need to reveal your team's weaknesses. Take it from someone who has undergone the same process many times: it is worth every headache, frustrating moment, and sleepless night. Now, are you ready to bring your team to the next level?

1
THE TURNOVER PROBLEM

Give your teachers the respect they deserve, because they are the ones who can help you get where you need to go.

—RICHARD HOWARD,
AMERICAN AUTHOR, LITERARY CRITIC,
TEACHER, AND TRANSLATOR

MAIN QUESTIONS

» Who is taking care of America's children?
» What are the characteristics of the child-care workforce and requirements for the job?
» What does it take to hire, retain, and promote committed professionals?
» What are the internal motivations to stay and grow in the industry?

Case Study: Turnover Trouble

Jen, a seasoned child-care director, posted an employment ad for a teaching position. A few days later, she received five applications from candidates who lacked any training or experience in the industry. She decided to contact them and schedule interviews. Only one of them showed up. In desperate need to fill the vacant position with a warm body that passed a background check, she hired the candidate to relieve her overworked staff. On the third day, the recruit did not show up for work.

THE EVOLVING BUSINESS OF CHILD CARE

Welcome to the reality of recruiting child-care professionals in the twenty-first century. From attracting qualified leads to hiring and onboarding, labor is the number-one organizational risk that child-care providers face. Regardless of the economic cycle, recruiting and retaining child-care professionals introduces particular challenges in every aspect of the process. As our society begins recognizing early childhood as an investment, administrators and teachers are held accountable for meeting quality standards to ensure the development of learning. Therefore, you must first identify the root causes of turnover to gain information so that you can develop a long-term recruiting strategy.

A well-educated workforce in early childhood strengthens the education pipeline. Yet, according to Katharine Stevens's *Workforce of Today, Workforce of Tomorrow: The Business Case for High-Quality Childcare*, a root cause of the problem in the United States is that we are underestimating the importance of the early years and the role early childhood professionals play in laying the foundation for learning.

In many states, child-care professionals are required to have a high school diploma and are not required to have experience before entering the industry. New recruits complete some training related to rules and regulations in early childhood education but generally do not receive much training with a pedagogical focus. Existing research has referred to low levels of qualifications among child-care workers and training that lacks coherence (see, for example, Center for the Study of Child Care Employment, 2018). This reality leads to possible confusion among providers, workers, and potential candidates about the education, training, and experience needed to be an effective child-care professional.

We cannot continue to underestimate the importance of early childhood educators and providers, because the business of child care is evolving from the traditional day-care setting into an education business. Current research demonstrates the significance of a child's first five years as a period in which the human brain develops faster than at any other time (see, for example, Center on the Developing Child, 2020; Pianta and Stuhlman, 2004). As we recognize the importance of learning environments and the quality of the workforce, this evolution is forcing operators to adapt to new expectations of what children are supposed to master before entering formal school and ways to provide that education.

In their blog post "There's No Going Back: Child Care after COVID-19," Rhian Evans Allvin, CEO of NAEYC, and Lauren Hogan, senior director of public policy and advocacy at NAEYC, state that child-care professionals must be recognized as essential workers. Many organizations are now advocating that those who are providing the service must be paid in alignment with the value of their work, skills, and competencies.

When I think of the image of the ideal preschool teacher, many great teachers come to mind. Let's take Mrs. Sammy as an example. Mrs. Sammy Canabal emigrated from Venezuela with a degree in sociology and earned her national child-development associate certification in the United States. At first, she worked as an assistant teacher and then as a lead teacher in a classroom for two-year-olds. At the end of her third year specializing in teaching toddlers, she requested to be transferred to the preschool section. It didn't take her long to recognize that there were many differences between the age groups and there was so much to learn. As an apprentice of veteran teacher Mrs. Susan Chow, she spent a couple of years studying preschoolers to understand the expectations. During this time, Mrs. Sammy observed a seasoned teacher develop individualized learning programs and teach children how to write and begin to learn how to read. During her second year in the preschool classroom, she conducted tandem training with Mrs. Chow. By the third year, she felt confident in teaching the class as a lead teacher. In all, it took Mrs. Sammy six years of her career as a teacher to master expectations, milestones, learning styles, and classroom management to ensure that children achieve positive outcomes.

Mrs. Sammy's experience reflects the reality that it takes a long time to master early childhood education. From the moment a child is born, there are several sequences of learning, growth spurts, and regressions that can be supported by a trained, skillful, and educated workforce. Skills such as potty training, classroom management, supporting development of eye-hand coordination, and teaching literacy take time, a lot of practice, and training.

In their book *High-Quality Early Childhood Programs: The What, Why, and How,* Laura Colker and Derry Koralek note that teachers in early childhood bring a variety of experiences and knowledge to their role with areas of strength and opportunities for growth. Some teachers are gifted in creating a program structure. Others are talented in guiding children's behavior. Therefore, supporting committed early childhood teachers in their journeys requires administrators and owners to provide professional-development opportunities and mentoring.

TERMS TO KNOW

- » **Onboarding:** the process of orienting and training a new employee
- » **Recruiting:** securing the services of; hiring
- » **Tandem training:** a coaching program designed to help a novice polish skills before teaching on her own
- » **Turnover:** people hired to replace those leaving a workforce

---

THE HIGHLY QUALIFIED EARLY CHILDHOOD EDUCATOR

Recruitment and retention of child-care workers begins with a deep understanding of the characteristics of the workforce and their internal motivations. What does it take to be an effective teacher? This was the question that researcher Laura Colker explored in her 2008 study and resulting article, "Twelve Characteristics of Effective Early Childhood Teachers." Colker surveyed early childhood educators representing a wide variety of backgrounds in terms of geographic location and experience to find out what attracted them to the field, the skills they value, and the rewards of the job. She identified the following characteristics of effective early childhood teachers:

- ▫ **Passion:** Feeling and belief that what they do matters to others; a high level of satisfaction with intrinsic features of the job, such as contact with children

- ▫ **Perseverance:** A determination to become a voice for young children as long-term advocates for improving children's lives

- **Willingness to take risks:** Eagerness to shake the status quo to achieve goals for children

- **Patience:** An understanding that not all children learn quickly but need time to practice repetitive skills

- **Flexibility:** Being comfortable with changing schedules and planned activities

- **Respect:** Able to show appreciation for diversity and hold the belief that everyone's life is enhanced by exposure to different people

- **Creativity:** Able to make learning fun and to meet learners where they are; able to overcome challenges, teach in a less-than-ideal physical environment, or make do with limited resources

- **Pragmatism:** An understanding of when to push and when to be patient; knowing which battles are winnable

- **Authenticity:** Truly liking young children and enjoying being with them

- **Love of learning:** Enthusiasm that inspires children to ask questions and try new things

- **High energy:** Willingness to dance, sing, get on the floor, and play

- **Sense of humor:** Able to incorporate fun and laughter as part of the classroom every day

THE RECRUITING STRUGGLE

Effective teachers share a combination of knowledge, skills, and personal characteristics. Nevertheless, attracting young professionals to become child-care workers is a very tough sell.

Developing a trained national workforce requires an strategic plan that involves a carefully crafted national marketing and recruitment strategy to change the low status and perception of the career from child-care worker to educator. By changing the perception of the role teachers play in the education pipeline, we are contributing to a new image of the profession.

I've dedicated the last fifteen years of my career to shaping the profile of the ideal child-care educator and trying to incorporate questions and experiences in the recruiting process that would allow our team to identify the personal characteristics of the ideal candidates in the early stages of the recruiting process.

Early childhood professionals such as Mrs. Sammy would not consider any other career. They love spending time with children and are lifelong learners. They are passionate about teaching young children—that is their personal commitment and biggest reward.

During periods of high economic growth, attracting workers to the industry is more challenging. Shortage of labor in child care intensifies because potential candidates can find higher pay, more benefits, and better working conditions in other less stressful work environments. Candidates can read between the lines in elaborate and carefully written job postings. They may ask themselves, who wants to chase twenty toddlers all day for twelve dollars an hour and no benefits? When you combine the requirements and responsibilities of the job with a modest salary, a lack of benefits, and few career-advancement opportunities, you are competing for the available talent with less stressful work environments. So what are your selling points as an employer? That is one of the answers we will address in the chapters on recruiting and designing the employees' journey.

According to a study by researchers Julia Torquati, Helen Raikes, and Catherine Huddleston-Casas, teachers who view the work as a career or a personal calling tend to stay in the industry. Early childhood professionals who view their job as emotionally and ideologically rewarding stay in the industry despite the low social status of the child-care profession. A pilot study by Elizabeth Russell, Sue Williams, and Cheryl Gleason-Gomez concluded that experienced married teachers are more likely to stay in the field. Perhaps this is the case because they belong to two-income households and can afford to take a lower-paying position.

But even dedicated child-care educators leave the profession. Let's review the literature devoted to the reasons child-care professionals leave the industry.

THE ROOT CAUSES OF TURNOVER

Turnover is a challenge faced by many organizations across all industries. As described in Jacob Morgan's article "The War for Talent Is Real: Here's Why It's Happening," a recent ManpowerGroup Talent Shortage Survey found that 38 percent of employers have difficulty filling jobs. In any industry, it is expensive to recruit, train, and onboard new employees. Yet, the difference is that in the child-care industry, employee turnover leads to long-lasting consequences. Children need a consistent and stimulating environment during the most critical years of brain development. With an industry average turnover that ranges from 30 to 40 percent, attracting, hiring, and educating candidates in the field of early childhood begins with the awareness of the consequences of turnover for young children and the need for valuing and respecting early childhood professionals.

A stable workforce complements family interactions, laying the foundation for competencies such as love for learning and social-emotional regulation. According to a 2004 working paper "Young Children Develop in an Environment of Relationships" from the Center on the Developing Child at Harvard University, children need nurturing and stable relationships with caring adults. Forming nurturing relationships is essential, beginning at birth.

When a staff member leaves, a child's ability to form trusting relationships is affected, leading to behavioral changes including regressions in some areas, confusion, and even sadness. The new teacher must work to create a trusting environment with the children and their families, establishing new classroom routines and implementing new classroom management during the adjustment period. It feels like starting the new school year all over again.

HOW TO CALCULATE YOUR EMPLOYEE TURNOVER RATE

The *employee turnover rate* is the percentage of employees who left a company within a certain period of time. Anja Zojceska explains in her 2018 article "HR Metrics: How and Why to Calculate Employee Turnover Rate" that you need three variables:

» The number of employees who left the company (both voluntarily and involuntarily) in a certain period of time

» The number of employees the company was employing at the beginning of that time period

» The number of employees the company was employing at the end of that time period

Voluntary turnover happens when an employee willingly leaves a company. Involuntary turnover happens when an employee is terminated due to poor job performance, absenteeism, or violation of workplace policies.

1. **Calculate your total number of employees.** This headcount should include all employees on the payroll. Do not include independent contractors or temporary workers who are on an

agency's payroll. Let's use the number of employees of ABC Learning Center as an example.

ABC Learning Center runs a headcount report monthly. The headcount on January 1 is 30 employees, on February 1 is 28 employees, and on March 1 is 30 employees.

2. Calculate the average number of employees. To calculate a monthly average, the next step is to add the total headcounts from each report together and then divide by the number of reports used to obtain the average number of employees on a payroll that month.

Add the three headcount totals: 30 + 28 + 30 = 88

Divide this sum to find the average headcount: 88 / 3 = 29.3

3. Calculate the number of employees who left the company. Make a list of the individuals with termination dates within the time period you are looking at. This list should include those who have left both voluntarily and involuntarily. Employees who are temporarily laid off, on furloughs, or have taken a leave of absence are not included, as they have not been terminated.

In late January, ABC Learning Center terminated 2 employees for cause.

4. Divide the number of separations by the average number of employees. Divide the number of separations in the time period by the average number of employees on the payroll in that time period.

ABC Learning Center had two separations and an average of 29.3 employees on the payroll: 2 / 29.3 = 0.068

5. Calculate the monthly turnover rate. Most employers report turnover rates as a percentage; therefore, you should multiply your answer from step 4 by 100.

0.068 x 100 = 6.8

ABC Learning Center's turnover rate for the month is 6.8 percent.

6. Calculate the annual turnover rate. Most employers want to report an annual turnover rate. To determine this, add the monthly turnover rates for the past twelve months together, then divide by twelve.

	JAN	FEB	MAR	APR	MAY	JUNE	JULY	AUG	SEP	OCT	NOV	DEC
Headcount	30	28	30	27	30	28	28	30	30	30	30	30
Separations	0	2	0	0	0	2	0	2	2	2	2	2
Turnover rate	0	6.8	0	0	0	6.8	0	6.8	6.8	6.8	6.8	6.8

ABC Learning Center's average number of employees per month is the total number of employees divided by twelve: 351 / 12 = 29.25.

Divide the number of separations by the average number of employees: 14 / 29.25 = 0.479.

Multiply 0.479 by 100 to get the annual turnover rate of 48 percent.

In her article "Turning Around Employee Turnover," Jennifer Robison cites a Gallup poll on reasons for employee turnover in companies:

- Managers influence at least 75 percent of the reasons for voluntary turnover. That means that the leading problem of turnover is the manager's leadership style or management approach.

- Lack of career advancement contributes to 32 percent of those voluntarily quitting jobs.

- Pay and benefits were the second most common answer (22 percent) as to why employees chose to leave.

- Of those who quit their jobs, 20.2 percent said they did so because they were not suited for that job or had the perception that they couldn't do what they do best every day.

- Much smaller percentages quit because of flexibility or scheduling (7.7 percent) or job security (1.7 percent).

DEVELOPING YOUR HIRING PROCESS

Developing an efficient and thorough hiring process is critical to your school's success.

In their article "The Balanced Scorecard—Measures that Drive Performance" for the *Harvard Business Review*, Robert Kaplan and David P. Norton assert that 80 percent of turnover stems from bad hiring decisions. If an employee is not suited to a position, the employee is unlikely to be successful. We will explore the employee journey in chapter 7.

Onboarding new employees is also critical to success. Employees need to understand your company's procedures, the company culture, and the training and mentoring opportunities new employees can expect. Directors who rush the onboarding process and fail to provide new recruits with mentorship opportunities are more likely to face lack of compliance with procedures and employees who do not feel that they are growing in their careers.

To attract and retain great teachers, you need to provide them with an environment that supports their personal and professional growth. Talent is attracted to organizations that are growing and promoting from within. Offering mobility inside your organization or professional-development opportunities is key to retaining employees. According to Jennifer Robison's article for Gallup, mobility does not necessarily mean moving up the corporate ladder. Many employees are searching for internal mobility—moving employees to new opportunities within the same company or opportunities for working on special projects, participating in mentorships, or shadowing other employees who have skills that the employees wish to learn. We will explore ideas for growing and developing talent in chapter 6.

Looking at Your Current Process

As a multisite operator, I experienced a period of high turnover rate, and I was determined to tackle it. According to some directors who reported to me, the most common reasons teachers left the industry were the salaries and the conditions of the job. That didn't entirely make sense to me, as new recruits knew the salary before accepting the position.

To understand the root causes and reverse the trend, our management team decided to conduct exit interviews and track termination data for an entire year. The data gathered from our findings indicated other warning signs completely unrelated to the salaries and working conditions. Some teachers were terminated because they didn't follow procedures or didn't understand the requirements or conditions of the job. Some had been recruited without any previous experience. Others hadn't received any type of training before starting the job, because directors needed to put a warm body in the classroom to comply with state ratios.

During the exit interviews, I had the chance to relate, connect, and understand the teachers' points of view. Here's a sample of the comments I received from departing employees:

- ☐ "Is easier to work at Walmart"

- ☐ "This is just a temporary job until I finish my career."

- ☐ "Too much drama working here"

I asked them for recommendations on how to retain passionate professionals so that we could design a process to create a pipeline to recruit, train, and promote the ideal educator. With the information we learned, we ended up reimagining the entire process to meet the expectations of a new generation of workers. The reasons why employees were leaving the company were not the ones I had thought they would be. Listening to frustrated teachers walk us through the different stages of the process allowed us to create an employee journey map. With that information, we were able to develop a new plan to change our internal processes and systems.

Let's review the findings of our exit interviews. Among the causes of employee turnover in the industry are wages, benefits, and working conditions. That was true for many of our employees who decided to leave. Take Mrs. Jamie, a devoted and committed child-care professional, as an example. Her salary did not keep pace with rising prices on her rent, groceries, and insurance. She constantly worried about how to make ends meet. Even though her salary had increased to sixteen dollars an hour, she still faced rising prices on her rent, so she had to find a roommate and supplement her salary with babysitting jobs. I have personally taken the time to give some financial-management classes to our employees, and I struggle to understand how they can make it without an additional income in the household.

Researchers Julia Torquati, Helen Raikes, and Catherine Huddleston-Casas state that early childhood educators are among the lowest-paid professionals in the United States. As I stated earlier, low wages are associated with higher staff turnover, which is known to be harmful to the development of children. According to the US Department of Labor, the median wages for child-care workers and preschool teachers average $11.65 per hour, which means that cooks and cashiers earn more in less stressful environments. In addition to that, very few employers offer benefits such as health insurance, retirement pensions, or paid educational opportunities.

However, higher wages and better benefits are costs that must be met through higher family tuition or government subsidies. Without government subsidies, the higher costs associated with this operating model will be passed on to families who are typically not able to afford them.

Exit interviews, which owners should conduct, allow you to follow the employee journey from hiring to termination to determine areas of opportunity. They also allow owners to see whether policies are being implemented consistently. Through our exit interviews, we learned that the main reason our teachers were leaving the industry was not the pay or benefits but inadequate administrative support. This finding aligns with research. A study described in the article "Teachers' Perceptions of Administrative Support and Antecedents of Turnover" by researchers Elizabeth Russell, Sue W. Williams, and Cheryl Gleason-Gomez found that teachers' intention to leave their current job was predicted by their perception of their director as a less supportive or unskilled administrator. Factors such as lack of consistency, scheduling, or the administrator's ability to create a positive culture that respects the value of their work were important factors associated with retention.

Leading child-care centers require administrators to empathize and support teachers. At times, all teachers need is encouragement and support. Working in a classroom full of vigorous toddlers is difficult, and once promoted, some administrators forget that it takes a special person to teach a group of young learners. Throughout my career, I have witnessed different leadership styles. On one end of the spectrum, I have heard directors answer a call from a toddler teacher with, "I'm sorry. We're short today. I'm not able to send a teacher to help you." On the other end of the spectrum, I have known directors who offer brain breaks to their teachers during stressful times.

Supporting her teachers during stress is one of the secrets of a high-performing director I know, Erika Seger. She says, "I never forgot how I felt when no one was there to support me during stressful times." Directors who stay connected to the classroom lead by example, stay grounded, and empathize with teachers so they can support the culture and create a positive environment in the workplace.

A key sign that turnover may be looming, as Jennifer Robison points out in her article, is when employees don't feel a connection to the organization's mission, purpose, or leadership. That is especially accurate in child-care settings when employees feel that there is a disconnect between the company's mission and its management practices. If your mission is "to provide a loving and caring environment" and management is not kind to staff members, employees will feel a disconnect with the organization's mission.

I once made the mistake of entering into a partnership with people with different management styles and priorities. In the end, there was so much tension and distrust in the partnership that I stopped having fun. That bad relationship in management was cascading throughout the organization without me saying a word. I was spending too much time fighting unnecessary battles. Out of respect to my team and the families, I made a bold decision to sell and start again. Yet, that negative experience provided me with many lessons on what it means to bring to life a company's mission and vision and the importance of aligning your values with others to be able to lead others. Leadership is a journey of self-reflection, self-awareness, and open communication that is shaped by the decisions you make every day to stay connected to the mission of your organization. Your organization's mission is not something you hang on a wall but something you practice each day.

BUILD YOUR KNOWLEDGE

» What are the characteristics of early childhood professionals?

» What are the requirements for the job?

» What are the qualities of teachers who tend to stay in the industry?

» What are the leading causes of turnover in child care?

2
THE CHILD-CARE ENTREPRENEUR

_GG_____

A business that needs an owner on a day-to-day basis is not a self-sustaining organism. It is a career.

—MARNIE FORESTIERI

MAIN QUESTIONS

» What are the keys to a successful child-care program?

» What risks do entrepreneurs assume when opening a child-care center?

» What is the ideal profile of a child-care entrepreneur?

» What are the main challenges directors face?

» What is the benefit of an owner's operations dashboard?

» What are examples of key performance indicators?

Case Study: The Owner-Director Dilemma

I have a dear friend who owns a successful independent child-care facility. Judith convinced her husband to invest in a child-care center, assuming huge risks including a loan to purchase a property. Judith ran the day-to-day operations for many years as the owner/director of the school. With an outstanding reputation in the community, her school markets itself. The families spread the word on her behalf on social media or off-line. She keeps in contact with graduating families and regularly posts success stories of former students who return to express how grateful they are for her influence during their early years.

A couple of years ago, Judith decided to step down and hire a director. In the beginning, it was difficult to delegate all the responsibilities. She would still talk to the employees, worry about the schedules, fret over billing, and answer parent concerns. The director she hired was always consulting her on the day-to-day operations.

One day, Judith and I started talking about her next goals. She enthusiastically shared that she was ready to start looking for a second location to grow her business. She had done an excellent job as the director of the facility and had achieved extraordinary accomplishments, including high-school-readiness scores. Yet, opening a second location would require Judith to learn to delegate.

Child-care entrepreneurs often complain about the difficulty of recruiting and motivating their employees; the lack of control over their own personal time; or things that are not working, such as increasing levels of parent complaints or employees not following procedures. If that describes you, to get renewed focus and excitement for your business or take your business to the next level, you need to learn how to streamline all your processes, take some time to understand the key components of high-quality care, hire the right people, communicate your vision, develop your processes, and then . . . let go.

Letting go is not easy but is necessary for your personal and business growth. Once you understand that the entity that you created must become a self-sustaining organism, you can begin to delegate tasks to help you elevate yourself. Elevating yourself means allowing yourself to grow to your next level or exploring your next venture. The first step is to delegate some areas of the business, clearly communicate the objectives, and create the systems to track performance.

Effective delegation leads to a culture of empowerment.

Like my friend Judith, you must decide to either pursue a career as an owner/director or to become a child-care entrepreneur. Dual-management systems in which directors report to the owner and teachers report to the director fail to promote a culture of empowerment and accountability across the organization. In that scenario, directors and teachers view the owner as the ultimate decision maker. Effective delegation, on the other hand, leads to a culture of empowerment.

The process begins with trusting the person you are delegating to and making intentional decisions to design systems and procedures to create an environment where directors can thrive. Once you have delegated responsibilities, you are ready to move to the back seat to monitor the most important aspects of your operations and to view your organization from a wide angle.

As for my friend Judith, she became a child-care entrepreneur. In her new role, she is constantly updating her facility, supporting her director, and monitoring her owner's dashboard. Owners such as Judith who understand that child care is a legacy business are able to reap what they sow. Like Judith, there are child-care owners around the country who proudly accept the responsibility of educating young children, reinvest in the quality of their programs, deeply care for their staff, and understand the challenges directors face in operations. They are building legacy businesses and supporting their communities one child at a time.

DO YOU HAVE WHAT IT TAKES TO BE A CHILD-CARE ENTREPRENEUR?

The ideal persona of a child-care entrepreneur is one who is hands-on, deeply cares about her staff and families, understands child development, and recognizes the operational challenges of the industry. The best child-care entrepreneurs are confident in their ability to deliver value to their customers, are motivated by a life purpose, demonstrate financial-management and leadership skills, empower directors, and form personal connections. Here are some questions to ask yourself: As a child, were you interested in babysitting or running a camp? Did you seek out entrepreneurial roles in school, in social organizations, or even in your previous job? A natural inclination of past interest in entrepreneurship and leadership roles seems to be a good indicator of potential future success. Here are signs that you are ready to become a child-care entrepreneur.

You are ready to break out of the corporate mindset. There are no prerequisites to becoming a child-care entrepreneur. If you're going to succeed in starting your own business, you'll have to break out of your corporate-employee mindset in which someone else controls your time and can direct your career. When you become an entrepreneur, you take control of your career and time, and you start seeing the world differently. Becoming an entrepreneur is a transition in which you create the conditions for others and adapt to market trends. Entrepreneurship is a journey that risk takers choose and is not meant for everyone. Child-care entrepreneurship is a rollercoaster of emotions—highs and lows that will set you on a path of impacting the lives in a community.

A life and purpose of helping children and families is important to you. Successful operators say no other business can match the personal satisfaction and the emotional rewards of child-care entrepreneurship. So before you open your doors, spend some time reflecting on your beliefs, your passions, your intentions for your new venture, and what your ideal child-care center would look like.

You are a people person, and you are ready to work hard. Having a child-care center is a lot of work and stress, especially during the pre-opening and start-up phases. Parents will be difficult. You will have trouble recruiting the right candidates. And children will cry. I remember vividly the first day at my first center. Every child was crying on their first day, new moms started crying when they dropped off their children, and one new teacher even packed her things because she could not control the children. It was complete chaos.

As the captain of the ship, you are expected to bring your team through the storm and stay in control to establish trust. The reality is that you can only create trust if everyone perceives that you are in control and you care. It has been a long time since that first day, and the same scene has repeated itself in every single center I've opened. Children, families, and staff members are adjusting to the new environment and forming trusting relationships. Being a people person will make it easier for you to understand the business side of the operation.

I once had a conversation with a multisite operator at a conference. He wanted to know the secrets of retaining staff members. He was complaining about the types of employees he was recruiting, high turnover, and a low level of engagement. I asked him about his recruitment and onboarding process. It didn't take me long to realize that he was an excellent financial person but not so much of a people person. He was seeing his organization through numbers, and it was very hard for me to explain to him the importance of intangibles. The best operators are passionate about people.

You can self-regulate and separate your personal life from your professional life. As a child-care operator, you are practically an extended family for the children. Parents will likely be very candid and open about what's going on at home. You're going to hear things that shouldn't be repeated. You have to be able to separate the professional and personal.

You can handle drama. The best way to describe the child-care entrepreneurship journey is to compare it to a reality show. New directors deal with entitlement and demands from employees. Gossip spreads like wildfire. It takes leadership to create a healthy culture, skills to handle gossips, and vision to navigate the drama. If you need a peaceful, drama-free environment to thrive, you will find child-care business ownership challenging.

You have basic knowledge about early childhood education. Understanding the education side of the business is critical and gives you a competitive advantage. Do you understand director certifications, state ratios, child development, and kindergarten-readiness expectations? The business side of your operations will be determined by your state regulations, such as the number of teachers you will need to operate the center or the purchases you have to make. Understanding the education side of the business gives you a better understanding of the operation issues your staff members will encounter and will give you credibility with your staff. Before opening your center, consider volunteering in a child-care center or enrolling in child-development classes to understand the rules and regulations of your state.

You have your finances in order and have a financial cushion. You are ready to start a business when you have income on which you can live comfortably while you build your business. You aren't going to be pulling a paycheck immediately. Furthermore, your past financial habits will likely to follow you into a business. If you are a big spender or you lack some financial accountability, you might not be ready to start a business.

You have a solid community. Here's the thing about starting a business: you can't do it by yourself. Before you take the leap of faith and start your program, you need to communicate your ambitions and goals to your family, friends, and loved ones. You will need their support.

You have a mentor. The best entrepreneurs have a mentor or an advisor they can lean on when looking for insight. This person can help guide you through the business questions and quandaries you will face.

Customer satisfaction score (CSAT): a metric that measures how happy your customers are

Key performance indicators (KPIs): a quantifiable measure used to evaluate the success of an organization, employee, and so on in meeting objectives for performance; the most important goals of your business; also called *business drivers*

Net promoter score (NPS): similar to KPI, this is a metric that calculates how likely a customer is to recommend your company or product

Retention rate: a metric used to see how many customers have stopped coming to your business or have cancelled their membership, subscription, or patronage. A high retention rate is good; it means you're keeping most of your clients and customers happy.

HOW TO DELEGATE AND ELEVATE

Once you decide to become a child-care entrepreneur, you will need to plan carefully to set up your team for success. Management teams are more important than the product or service offered. Successful business owners have some things in common:

- **compelling visions** for their organizations,

- **great teams in place** that share their core values,

- **reliance on data** to manage their business regularly, and

- **design processes** to ensure that every aspect of the operation is followed consistently.

Organizing and Focusing with Dashboards

A dashboard is like an aircraft flight-control system. Once the pilot takes off in the aircraft, the main responsibility is to check whether the plane is heading in the right direction. During the flight, the pilot might allow the copilot to take control of the aircraft but is always monitoring if the course changes by a disturbance such as the wind.

Similarly, an *operations dashboard* allows you to create a scorecard to monitor critical business processes and activities. A dashboard, as defined by New Age Leadership, "is a talent management tool that allows an employee (usually a mid- to senior-level leader) to find out how others perceive her. As human beings, it is virtually impossible to see ourselves completely objectively. This tool allows leaders to see the gap between their own self-perception and how others view the leader." (There are many free resources available online, such as 360 Degree Feedback at https://newageleadership.com/360-degree-feedback/) Just like an aircraft flight-control system, your dashboard allows you to obtain timely information to measure, monitor, and manage your business. When a disturbance occurs, you have to be able to take control to steer your organization in the right direction. A well-designed operations dashboard allows you to track front-end activities, such as sales, customer service, and marketing, as well as back-end processes, such as finance, human resources, and classroom management.

There are many benefits to using operations dashboards. They allow owners to communicate their expectations in metrics and use data to manage their business, as well as break the strategic plan into small tactical plans. A dashboard is a simple document or technology interface that allows you to monitor the most important business metrics of your child-care business to make sure everyone is moving in the same direction.

When I started out in the industry, I invested years obtaining the credentials to understand child development and center operations. The time spent in the classrooms provided me with insights on day-to-day issues teachers and directors face, such as trying to put children to sleep during nap time, scheduling, and managing behavioral problems. After gaining a deep understanding of child-care operations, I am able to sort potential problems into categories to pinpoint the ones that are critical to the organization. At this stage of my career, I also have a clear image of the ideal profile of a child-care entrepreneur. What I have learned is that owners do not need to know every detail of what happens inside the school. They just need to understand the most important issues that are critical to the school's long-term success.

I created my first operations dashboard out of frustration. A biting problem in the toddler room started it. The same child would repeat the same unwanted behaviors every day. The director I hired to replace me was coming back to me over and over with this problem. I patiently walked her though the process to address it; yet, the biting issue was becoming a huge customer-service problem. As a solution, I wrote down the entire procedure and added it to the director's handbook, giving her very specific instructions on how to handle the situation. I also added the same procedure to the parent handbook. That didn't help. In this case, I had recruited an excellent teacher and turned her into an unhappy director. The responsibility for dealing with the problem was still coming back to me. (The good news is that if I hadn't gone through all this, I wouldn't be writing this book.)

To address the biting problem, I decided to make my approach visible and coach the director, as she did not feel comfortable discussing the situation with the parents. The first operations dashboard included the number of incident reports regarding this problem. I also gave the director a journal for her to use to track the steps she took to handle the situation as well as her progress. In a matter of a couple of weeks, I started seeing the number of incidents drop. By delegating and measuring that specific number, I was able to translate the importance of customer service to the director and help her follow the same procedures I would follow. I maintained a strategic level without having to handle the responsibility personally.

Together, my team and I developed methods for handling most of the issues we encounter. By now, we've solved all sorts of potential problems in child-care settings, from dealing with custody battles to handling a disease outbreak to bad hiring decisions and everything in between. Our team is now committed to sharing what we have learned with the new generation of child-care administrators and entrepreneurs.

When I started my operations dashboard, I realized that I could communicate strategy in very simple terms to my director. The dashboard allowed me to communicate the goals; identify potential risks; and break down the strategic goals by week, month, or quarter. By now, my chief of operations and I have developed a solid relationship that makes me think that sometimes she can read my mind. We share the same values, work hard, and trust each other in a culture of respect, loyalty, empowerment, and growth.

As a director, she created her own dashboard to communicate with her direct reports her expectations and to assign tasks by week, month, and quarter. We organized our managerial processes, job descriptions, and expectations all under one framework. Later on, we figured out that we could tie the dashboard to compensation, budgeting planning, and feedback to the original dashboard.

My first operations dashboard was a simple spreadsheet with my most important indicators in every area of the business. As time passed, we developed a technology interface. I included all our operations metrics to measure, such as the amount billed, leads generated, and the payroll ratio. On a monthly basis, I wanted to measure the children's assessments, classroom checklists, and employee turnover rate. On a bimonthly basis, I wanted to measure the parent surveys and employee satisfaction reports, as well as surveys in which employees were able to give us feedback on our work as administrators.

Child-care owners face the same challenges regardless of the size of their operations. Take Chris, as an example. His biggest challenge as a multisite operator is that directors keep coming to him with day-to-day operations questions. That is the same problem Elizabeth, a single-unit operator, faces. When a director struggles to deal with the same problems and situations over and over, that might be a sign that either the owner still has some homework to do or that the director needs coaching or more experience. Directors who seem overwhelmed and in emergency mode most of the time are probably not a good fit if an owner is new to child-care operations. In contrast, high-performing directors run centers so smoothly that they spend most of their time in strategic activities.

Let's face it. In some instances, you might hire a director who is not the right fit, or a director may quit. That's one of the reasons you need a recruiting strategy for directors. If, as an owner, you're performing some of the day-to-day tasks of a director, that is a clear indicator that your director might need coaching in some areas or might not be the right candidate for the job.

If you are spending time trying to figure out how to help your director recruit and manage staff members or handle customer issues, it's time to walk you through the process of creating your first strategic operations dashboard. The process begins by understanding the critical aspects of your child-care business to be able to identify strategic objectives and design procedures to effectively delegate and respond to frequently asked questions or situations.

Here are common examples that might indicate that you still have some homework to do as an owner. Your director is repeatedly struggling with the same issues and questions, such as, "I need to repair a toilet," "Can I buy a hundred dollars' worth of supplies?" "Bobby in the toddler room bit again. What should I do?" "One of my teachers quit," "My teachers are coming in late most days," or "I am having trouble recruiting teachers."

CREATING DASHBOARDS

Dashboards alert users about risks and allow them to predict potential problems before they happen. Let's start by understanding the different operations dashboards: operational, tactical, and strategic.

- ▣ An **operational dashboard** allows **teachers** to manage and control their classrooms.

- ▣ A **tactical dashboard** allows the **director** to monitor projects or departments within the school, such as the marketing department, curriculum, and operations.

- ▣ A **strategic dashboard** (also called the **owner's** operations dashboard) works for single-unit and multisite operations, as well as franchisees.

Let's go back to the directors' common problems and situations. The dashboard will help the director manage the problem on her own or decide whether to consult the owner. Generally, the director will manage a tactical problem; the owner will manage a strategic problem.

PROBLEM	POSSIBLE SOLUTION(S)	STRATEGIC OR TACTICAL?
"I need to repair a toilet."	Check the maintenance log, review procedures, and refer to the approved vendor list to find a plumber.	Tactical
"Can I buy a hundred dollars' worth of supplies?"	Allocate a supply budget for the month.	Tactical
"Bobby in the toddler room bit again. What should I do?"	Refer to the discipline policy in the parent handbook.	Tactical
"One of my teachers quit."	Refer to the human-resources manual. Perform a staff-satisfaction survey, or refer to that data if she already has surveyed the staff to get an idea of the source of the problem.	Tactical
"My teachers are coming in late most days."	Refer to the human-resources manual. Perform a staff-satisfaction survey, or refer to that data if she already has surveyed the staff to get an idea of the source of the problem.	Tactical
"I am having trouble recruiting teachers."	Craft a new hiring procedure, in consultation with the owner.	Strategic
"I am having trouble getting leads to visit the center."	Review your advertising campaign.	Strategic
"I am having trouble closing sales after tours."	Review your tour checklist and procedures.	Strategic

Try it for yourself. Make three columns on a piece of paper. In the first column, list the most common situations at your center. Next, brainstorm possible solutions and list those in the second column. Then, identify whether the problem is a tactical or strategic issue. There are some areas that you need to track regularly, and other areas that are not as important. For example, if your director is receiving customer complaints about misbehaviors in the classroom, you might need to track incident reports to monitor customer-service issues, as families might disenroll from the program if policies are not implemented consistently. If you are not able to brainstorm a possible solution or delegate the task to your director, that means that the situation needs a strategy or planning session.

Sample of an Owner's Operations Dashboard

WEEKLY GOALS	MONTHLY GOALS	QUARTERLY GOALS
Amount billed	Children assessments, documentation, and classroom reports	Parent surveys Customer-service metrics
Disenrollment and reason	Financial ratios review and projections	Employee surveys 360-degree surveys
Financial ratios	Licensing reports	Employee professional-development plans and budget.
Lead-to-tour conversions	Turnover rate and exit interviews	
Website traffic metrics, social-media tracking, and Google analytics	Enrollment projections	
Payroll as a percent of revenue	Employee experience survey (recruiting, onboarding, mentoring)	
	Center occupancy	
	SWOT meeting	

How to Create Your Owner's Strategic Dashboard

The principle is simple: what you measure is what you get. In 1992, Robert Kaplan and David Norton introduced the balanced scorecard concept in their article "The Balanced Scorecard—Measures that Drive Performance" in the *Harvard Business Review*. The authors discussed measuring performance across more perspectives than merely the financial and presented a solution that includes human issues. As of today, the balanced scorecard ranks as one of the most powerful management tools.

Unfortunately, the child-care industry lacks a comprehensive, interactive software or reporting system. Therefore, child-care providers have to rely on different reports and software solutions to create an owner's strategic dashboard. To gather the important metrics for your operations, you need information from several sources:

- ⊡ Your customer relationship management (CRM) system or process

- ⊡ Your accounting system

- ⊡ Your billing software

- ⊡ Your curriculum-and-assessment software

- ⊡ Your parent-communication software

- ⊡ Surveys of customer or employee feedback

Are you ready to become the pilot of the plane, set up the destination, and use the control panel to put the airplane on autopilot?

Step 1: Complete Your Strategic and Tactical Goal Chart

The process of building your dashboard begins by identifying your strategic objectives. Owners typically spend a few days or weeks crafting the organization's strategy and then pass it to the director to figure out how to implement it. The reality is that, after passing it along, nothing happens. Wayne Eckerson, author of *Performance Dashboards: Measuring, Monitoring, and Managing Your Business*, says that developing a strategic dashboard changes the process, as it provides both a communication tool and a way to measure progress.

Once you complete your vision, write your mission statement, and list your values, you are ready to set goals and objectives for every department. (Note: I offer a thorough explanation of how to do this in chapter 5 of my first book in this series, *The Basics of Starting a Child-Care Business*.) Owners should offer a very clear direction from the top of what you want to measure—your business drivers. Business drivers are the most important goals of your organization, your KPIs, such as:

- ⊡ Sales—waiting list for enrollment

- ⊡ Financial—growth in revenue

- ⊡ Customer service and retention—high customer satisfaction, best school-readiness scores

- ⊡ Human resources—low staff-turnover rates, best place to work

- ⊡ Licensing—perfect licensing track record

◉ Marketing—lead generation, percentage of market share

For our discussion, let's consider this strategic goal for sales: "Have an enrollment waiting list in the first year." To achieve this goal, you need to break down your strategy into smaller weekly and monthly goals. To achieve your enrollment goals, you need to take certain action steps, such as giving several tours to get the expected enrollments. Let's say your license capacity is 150. You enroll 54 children prior to opening, so you have a 96 spots to fill in 12 months; therefore, your tactical goal is to enroll 8 students per month. To achieve that goal, you need leads or people interested in taking a tour. Let's say that you can enroll 50 percent of the families who take a tour at your school. By tracking your lead-to-tour conversions, you have an idea of how many leads you need to get someone to book a tour and how many tours you need to give to enroll someone that month. Therefore, your action step is to get 4 tours per week to enroll 2 students the following week.

STRATEGIC GOAL	MONTHLY	WEEKLY	ACTION STEP
Have enrollment waiting list in the first year	8 enrollments	2 enrollments	You need to give 4 tours every week or 16 every month.

Step 2: Write Your Vision and Business-Plan Objectives in the Present Tense

"A picture is worth a thousand words." This saying by advertising executive Fred R. Barnard is applicable to your business. Describing a powerful vision for the future, your company sets the expectations and helps you communicate them to your direct reports. Your owner's dashboard also allows you to efficiently communicate your goals and create agreement between you and your director. Sharing your vision is an important part of your director's onboarding training. Go back to the vision and objectives of your business plan. Write it in the present tense, as it is already happening. The following is an example of a powerful vision statement, redrafted in the present tense, constructed from the chart below.

DEPARTMENT	STRATEGIC GOAL	VISION
Sales	Have a waiting list in the first year	Our center will be operating at full capacity, and we will have a waiting list.
Marketing	Become the market leader in the community	We will be the market leader, and families will be our advocates in the community.
Licensing	Have a perfect licensing record	We will have an outstanding reputation in the community for perfect kindergarten-readiness scores and a perfect licensing record.

Finance	Achieve profitability and efficiency; invest in what we value	We will operate efficiently, have increased our cash reserves for emergencies, and achieve our ROI for investors.
Human Resources	Be considered the best place to work	Our turnover rate will be less than 10 percent this year.
Customer Service and Retention	Have high customer satisfaction and excellent customer-service experiences	Customers will be our advocates.
Operations	Have an outstanding reputation in the community	Our classroom management scores will be consistently over 90 percent. Classroom inspections and safety procedures will be followed at all times. We will start the accreditation process.

Our center is operating at full capacity. Our waiting list is increasing. We are the market leader and considered the best place to work. Families are our advocates in the community. We have an outstanding reputation for perfect kindergarten-readiness scores, are working to obtain our accreditation, and have a perfect licensing record. We operate efficiently, have built out cash reserves for emergencies, and met the return on investment (ROI) expectations for our investors.

Step 3: Create Your Tactical Goals

Your business plan offers a way to quantify your goals to meet your financial projections. After writing your strategic goals—the big picture—you are ready to match your business-plan objectives to your business goals. Let's complete the tactical goals column of the graph.

DEPARTMENT	STRATEGIC GOAL	TACTICAL GOALS
Sales	Have a waiting list in the first year	Enroll 8 students per month
Marketing	Become the market leader in the community	• Increase the web page authority (how high the pages of your website rank when searched by potential customers) by 20 percent in the first year • Generate 20 leads per month with marketing campaign • Have 5 leads referred by families per month
Licensing	Have a perfect licensing record	No write-offs or violations
Finance	Achieve profitability and efficiency; invest in what we value	Payroll-to-income percentage is lower than 45 percent

Human Resources	Be considered the best place to work	• Turnover rate does not exceed 10 percent
		• Employee satisfaction is 90 percent
		• 360-degree reviews (from peers, customers, and managers) are over 90 percent
Customer Service and Retention	Have high customer satisfaction and excellent customer-service experiences	Customer-service metrics, such as CSAT, are over 90 percent
Operations	Have an outstanding reputation in the community	• Test scores of students are at or above 90 percent
		• Safety procedures are followed
		• Accreditation status has been achieved

Step 4: Create a List of Ideas for Each Tactical Goal

Dale Carnegie, writer and lecturer on salesmanship and corporate training, said, "People support a world they help create." That quote serves as a reminder of the importance of involving your director in developing your ideas and timeline for action steps and in assigning the owner of each goal. The director needs to be involved in the process to effectively delegate the task. Even if you already know the action steps, the process of involving or asking your director for feedback allows your director to support the world she is helping create. You can do this by asking open-ended questions such as the following:

▣ What actions steps should you take to obtain a perfect licensing record?

▣ What are some strategies to engage your employees?

▣ What are some action steps to plan to improve your employee experience?

With your director, brainstorm ideas for achieving each of your strategic and tactical goals. One way to do this is to record each idea on a sticky note. Using sticky notes allows you to visualize your ideas that you can share. For example, our team uses this method to organize projects, examine customer journeys, look at employee experiences, and create timelines.

1. Draw a grid on an easel pad. You can use the grid to make a calendar, timeline of events, a customer journey, or an employee experience.

2. Jot down a specific idea, action step, or task on a sticky note.

3. Place each note on the grid in a sequence or order of priority.

Let's say you are conducting a delegation session on customer-service expectations, with the goal of having high customer satisfaction. Instead of telling your director that you expect everyone to be friendly or attentive, you can choose to involve her in the process. By collaborating with your director, you are creating accountability and delegating the responsibility.

First, create a shared vision. Start by stating the strategic and tactical goals: have high customer satisfaction by offering an excellent customer-service experience. Collaborate with your director in identifying what experiences would be considered excellent and what expectations there should be. Write each expectation on a separate sticky note. Next, conduct a brainstorming session in which you and your director jot down your different buyer personas or types of customers: potential customer, existing customer, customer with more than one child enrolled, and so on. Then brainstorm ideas for each customer type's goals and objectives. Remind your director that you are looking for volume of ideas, not quality. At this point in the discussion, anything counts!

Share your sticky notes with each other, and identify the scenarios to shape a common vision. For example, brainstorm ideas and images of quality customer service, such as a welcoming reception area, asking parents to complete a questionnaire before the tour, inviting prospective families to meet the classroom teachers, having friendly staff members greet prospective families during the tour, and having the director offer to answer questions and follow up with families the day after the tour.

Once you have brainstormed ideas for your shared vision, your team is ready for the next step. Sketch out a timeline that includes customer touchpoints in the customer journey, and organize the sequence from the moment the prospective parent enters the building to follow up and everything in between, such as interactions, following up after a tour, completing enrollment forms, greeting the family on the first day, meeting the teacher, and so on. Organize the sequence in a grid or a timeline to create a visual of the customer journey.

Next, take a look at the journey, and mark potential roadblocks in the process. For example, the director is giving an information tour and stops by the toddler classroom to meet the teacher. She finds the classroom in complete chaos. Of course, that parent would not enroll his child. Instead of pointing out the problem directly (the teacher needs to get her classroom under control), the director invites the teacher to become part of the customer-experience discussion and to help map the overall customer experience, including the touchpoint of a parent visiting her classroom. This gives the teacher ownership of the touchpoint and allows her to collaborate on solutions.

Step 5: Create Your List of Action Steps

Once you select your tactical goals and map your ideas, you are ready to add action steps, such as the following:

- How many tours must you give every week to have a waiting list by the end of the year? Who will conduct the tours?

- What are the steps to take following a tour? Who will do these tasks?

- How will you measure the progress?

- What is your budget for this action step?

The list of tasks become action steps. By involving your director in the process, you are delegating the tasks and creating accountability. The strategic and tactical goals columns of the graph allow you to communicate and quantify your vision.

DEPARTMENT	STRATEGIC GOAL	TACTICAL GOALS	ACTION STEPS	PERSON(S) RESPONSIBLE	MEASUREMENT	BUDGET
Sales	Have a waiting list in the first year	Enroll 8 students per month	• Give 4 tours every week. • Develop a process to follow up with leads every Wednesday. • Organize meet-the-teacher event prior to child starting the program. • Create community-outreach program.	Director	Monthly enrollments	
Marketing	Become the market leader in the community	• Increase the web page authority by 20 percent in the first year • Generate 20 leads per month with marketing campaign • Have 5 leads referred by families per month	• Conduct a consumer-awareness campaign • Calculate lead conversion (how many leads visit the center and how many enroll) • Set marketing-budget ratio goals • Look at the return on the marketing investment • Calculate the total cost of customer acquisition	Owner	Lead-to-tour conversion rate	2 percent of budget
Licensing	Have a perfect licensing record	No write-offs or violations	Conduct weekly inspection	Director	Results of every inspection visit	

Category	Objective	Metric	Action	Owner	Frequency
Finance	Achieve profitability and efficiency; invest in what we value; have effective cash-flow management and a financial control dashboard	Have payroll-to-income percentage lower than 45 percent	Track weekly payroll report	Owner	Payroll ratio; for example, if your total billing for the month is $100,000 and you spent $60,000 on payroll, your payroll ratio is 60 percent
Human Resources	Be considered the best place to work	• Turnover rate does not exceed 10 percent • Employee satisfaction is 90 percent • Create a pipeline of candidates • 360-degree reviews are over 90 percent	• Create internship program • Conduct employee-experience survey	Director	Bimonthly
Customer Service and Retention	Have high customer satisfaction and excellent customer-service experiences	Customer-service metrics, such as CSAT, are over 90 percent	Respond to customer complaints within 1 hour	Director	Results of CSAT
Operations	Have an outstanding reputation in the community	• Test scores of students are at or above 90 percent • Safety procedures are followed • Accreditation status has been achieved	• Review test scores • Conduct professional development on curriculum • Conduct inspections • Review safety paperwork	Director	As needed Weekly

Now it's your turn. Meet with your director to complete the strategic and tactical goals columns. Create the timeline of the action steps and decide who is responsible for completing them, determine how you will measure your progress, and set the budget.

The framework you create with your director will become the foundation of your job description and cascade throughout your organization chart. An owner needs buy-in from a director in the same way a director requires buy-in from the rest of the team. In the following chapter, you will learn how to create operations dashboards for your director and your teachers.

Step 6: Monitor Your Progress

Successful child-care centers share the same vision of quality, quantify results, and reward employees based on those results. Owners need to track to evaluate whether their actions are driving the desired outcomes. The keys to quality are consistency in following processes and monitoring results to create accountability.

The best way to monitor results is to use the framework of the dashboard during your weekly meetings. Measures without meetings are useless. This is the opportunity to ask your director specific questions related to your goals and action steps, such as, "What are you doing about this number?" or "What could you do to avoid this situation next time?"

Weekly Meeting Agenda

	TACTICAL GOAL	ACTUAL RESULTS
Sales		
Marketing		
Licensing		
Finance		
Human Resources		
Customer Service and Retention		
Operations		

Step 7: Analyze Your Data

Once you track and gather your data from all your KPIs, you can examine the information to identify trends and patterns. For example, if your monthly turnover rate is going up and your employee satisfaction scores are going down, that might be an indicator that there is a problem in your human-resources department. If you are not getting enough leads from your marketing initiatives, there may be a problem with your marketing campaign or setup. Or if you are getting many leads and tours but they are not converting to sales, this could be a sign that your sales process is not working. Your data will provide you with strategic feedback to adapt and create new action steps to steer the organization in a new direction.

Step 8: Share and Reflect with the School Team

Communicating your objectives to the rest of the school team creates a culture of measurement. For example, you could share your latest customer-satisfaction results, classroom monthly reviews, or group aggregations of children's assessments and progress reports. Sharing your data sends the message across the organization that you want to promote accountability at all levels. This approach allows all employees to understand objectives and how to use measures so they can establish their own objectives. When you tie your measures to your promotions, recognitions, and awards, you are sending a very clear message of what your expectations are.

Once you create the top-level strategy scorecard, you are ready to let the strategy cascade to other parts of the organization. Involve the users to align everyone to the strategy. Once the business metrics for the owner strategic dashboard is completed, you can create and transfer the tactical dashboard to the director's dashboard. (We will design the director's dashboard in chapter 5.) Yet, to create a culture of accountability, operations dashboards have to cascade throughout the organization to include teachers' and assistants' operations dashboards. We will discuss these in chapter 7.

BUILDING A CULTURE THAT PROMOTES ACCOUNTABILITY, MEASUREMENT, AND COLLABORATION

Use your dashboards to guide discussions during your weekly and operational review meetings. Every meeting, ask the owners of the dashboards to stand up and share their metrics, such as how much they have billed, disenrollment, operational risks, and turnover.

The process is designed to create a culture of measurement, accountability, and collaboration in which the team determines the priorities and how to allocate funds to support initiatives or areas of concern. If the team identifies a potential roadblock, they can brainstorm ideas and then transfer that problem to a planning board.

Consider the following example. Absenteeism has become a problem in recent weeks. Teachers are calling out at an alarming rate. The director needs the team's help in identifying the root cause of the problem and developing a strategy to address the issue. In the following chapter, we will review how to conduct a planning session with the team.

BUILD YOUR KNOWLEDGE

- » What are the keys to the success of a child-care program?
- » What risks do entrepreneurs assume when opening a child-care center?
- » What is the ideal profile of a child-care entrepreneur?
- » What are the main challenges directors face?
- » What is the benefit of an owner's dashboard?
- » What are examples of KPIs?
- » Create your first owner's dashboard grid.

3
CRAFTING THE CULTURE OF YOUR ORGANIZATION

_❝❝_____

Children's joy in learning and the teacher's caring demeanor are signs that this program has an intentional plan for excellence on standards of quality.

—LAURA COLKER AND DERRY KORALEK, *HIGH-QUALITY EARLY CHILDHOOD PROGRAMS*

MAIN QUESTIONS

» What are the symptoms of a bad culture?

» What are the key components of a high-quality program?

» What are common shapers of culture?

» What are the signs of a toxic culture?

» What are major sources of satisfaction and frustration in a school?

» What are some things that owners and directors do that are teamwork terminators?

» Why is it important to align the vision of your organization?

» What are the elements of a great culture?

» How can you rebuild your organization after COVID-19?

» What are the biggest challenges directors face during COVID-19?

Case Study: School Culture Reflects Owner Values

A school culture reflects the owner's values, motivations, and purpose. I once tried to explain to a new child-care owner that his business plan was unrealistic and would put a lot of pressure on the director and set her up for failure. The owner had a finance background, and his goal was to enroll one hundred children in the first six months of opening his school in a highly saturated market. He explained that he had developed an attractive cash-incentive bonus for the director based on enrollment numbers and was planning to offer discounts for new families.

As a former director, I could just imagine the type of culture that the sales incentive would create. The value proposition of this program was a state-of-the-art facility with discounted child care. When the team did not meet the numbers, he had to let half of the staff members go, setting up a program culture of putting profits over people.

Owners tend to hire candidates who align with their core values and leadership style. In an owner-operator model, a business owner recruits a director to manage the operations, implement cultural guidelines, and communicate the vision. That means that the owner needs to be able to transfer the vision and cultural expectations across the organization through the director and make the director accountable for setting the expectations.

In certain cases, owners have partners, and that relationship will define the culture of the organization. I've heard too many stories of entrepreneurs falling into the trap of creating partnerships that fall apart: friends who enter into a partnership agreement to open a child-care business only to later find out that they have different sets of values or visions for the company; couples who invest in a child-care business and later start fighting for control; and franchisees who enter a franchise system that does not meet their expectations. Partnerships are formed because people might have complimentary skills. Yet, according to Philip Thurston in his article for the *Harvard Business Review*, "When Partners Fall Out," the control and culture of the company is threatened when partners grow to dislike and distrust each other.

Entrepreneurship is a long ride, and founders are responsible for setting clear expectations of who is in charge from the beginning. As a child-care founder, you are responsible for setting the culture and must keep in mind that the signs of a bad partnership will cascade throughout the organization. Many of the symptoms of a bad culture will impact the entire organization: your recruitment and marketing strategy, your operations, and even your profitability.

Experts recommend never setting up a partnership in which two or more people have equal ownership and power in decision making. If you are already in a situation like this in which you are fighting unnecessary battles with partners, it will be difficult to offer your team the culture they deserve. Some of the warning signs that a partnership is not working include not trusting that your partner is capable, no longer believing that the company has a future, or judging your partner's code of ethics. You have to be able to enjoy the entrepreneurship ride to create the culture your team and families deserve. Your director and your team need a leader capable of providing clear direction and having a personal commitment to support a culture of success.

DEFINING A SCHOOL CULTURE

School culture is an intangible that can be hard to explain; yet, culture is the foundation of excellence and long-term success. Sales-driven cultures lead to low employee engagement, customer churn, unhappy employees, and high turnover rates. These organizations attract customers who are difficult to please, leaving owners wondering what they are doing wrong. Reaching profitability is a goal but should not be the main message. As Jacob Morgan points out in *The Employee Experience Advantage*, the main message starts at the top of the organization and is the foundation upon which employee experience is built.

All organizations have a culture. Sometimes owners create it intentionally, and sometimes it develops over time to reflect the values of the owners. In my experience, the culture always comes back to the heart of the owner or the leadership team of the company. Child care can be a profitable industry if done right. Nevertheless, I believe that companies and entrepreneurs entering the business solely for profits do not have a sustainable business plan. Companies and owners whose main focus is on increasing revenues send a clear message to employees on what is most important. Owners who operate successful centers but cut expenses on food, supplies, or payroll also send a strong message: quality is not important. A culture of profit starts taking shape organically, and employees who don't fit into that culture will leave. The effects of a culture of profit trickle down throughout the entire organization: employees are not engaged, there is a high turnover rate, the quality of instruction is low, and there is lousy customer service. I have witnessed the rise and the fall of many child-care centers. A parent who has had a bad experience will end up telling eight to nine people. When many families in the community share negative experiences, there is no marketing budget that can fix the bad reputation that the center develops.

I once visited a state-of-the-art facility in Texas operating at 30 percent capacity while its competitors were operating at capacity. I was intrigued by their low enrollment numbers and wanted to learn the reason a new facility was struggling. I asked a business owner in the community and learned that the facility had absentee owners residing in another state and that the director and some staff members had left the school due to disagreements with management. As a consequence, even though the facility had a new director, the school was struggling to attract families.

In contrast, programs that are built around the key ingredients of high-quality learning and that set realistic expectations are built for long-term success. Eileen Ramos from Planet Learning in Orlando illustrates the character traits of a successful owner. Eileen leads by example. To achieve the goals of her business plan, she recruits like-minded, purpose-driven directors and teachers. The moment you walk into her school, you experience what a high-quality learning environment offers: happy teachers, happy children, and happy parents. She knows each employee by name, sets the program expectations, and creates an experience for each employee. (We will explore creating the director experience in chapter 5.) High-performing directors will only follow a leader like Eileen, who has a well-articulated purpose. The purpose, in turn, leads to commitment to procedures and best practices, shared leadership, and community. Everyone in the team is propelled to become the best version of themselves.

TERMS TO KNOW

Culture: the values, motivations, and purpose of an organization

Employer branding: how prospective employees perceive a company

Employee engagement: the passion, commitment, and enthusiasm that employees have for a company and their role in it

Value proposition: an aspect of a company, such as a feature, innovation, or service, that makes it attractive to customers

---

THE SECRET OF SUCCESSFUL SCHOOLS

Over the years, I have met successful child-care owners with great visions and purpose who inspire their teams to create communities of learning. I have also met owners struggling to understand why their centers have large turnover rates, customer issues, a lack of procedures, and low satisfaction scores among families and staff.

Business plans include lots of information, such as management, marketing, and operations sections. Yet, what a business plan fails to convey is what actually makes a school successful: the intangibles, the culture. The cultural environment isn't something you can touch or taste; it's the vibe of a school. Author Jacob Morgan defines it this way: "From an employee's perspective, it is the feeling in the pit of your stomach when you don't want to go to work or the excitement you get from wanting to go to work." In a service business, the culture of the organization will determine how employees get their jobs done. Entrepreneurs should recognize its importance because the symptoms of a bad culture will impact the entire organization, from recruitment to the marketing strategy to operations to profitability.

In child care, a toxic culture is plagued with drama, gossip, high rates of absenteeism and turnover, unhappy employees, and bad employee reviews. Employees do not really want to work there; they just have to. If you are exhibiting some of the warning signs of a toxic child-care culture, it might be time to assess your organization's cultural well-being to identify root causes. It's just a matter of time until a competitor will enter the market to rescue families and teachers from a toxic culture.

We once opened a new school at full capacity only to later find out that we were not necessarily a recognized brand in the community or even perceived as a better child-care option. The main reason we were in demand was that competitors in the community offered terrible customer service. For this particular school, it had taken me five years to negotiate a land deal with a successful developer. Even though I was concerned about the demographic report, which showed that the area did not have the needed number of children in the community to sustain a new center, I was completely convinced about our vision. When we finally opened, I was surprised. We opened a new school in the middle of December at full capacity.

The owners of competing child-care centers in the community had become arrogant with the illusion of extensive waiting lists, so they offered parent tours only once a year. Their customer service did not meet the needs of the families they served. The moment that an unknown competitor opened, those recognized brands lost half of their enrollment. The families who enrolled at our center shared how they really wanted to leave and how teachers did not want to work there.

The reality is that a culture of excellence is the most powerful marketing differentiator, an idea we will explore in depth in the third book of this series. Prospective families can experience the culture of a school just by walking into the facility. Teachers are happy and engaged. Children are smiling. Owners are committed and caring, even if they don't have an available spot, because they understand their role of supporting the families in their community.

Quality is a process that is reflected at all levels of your center and starts with you. Owners and leadership teams who make team building, high-quality instruction, performance, and customer experiences the core mission of the organization build profitable businesses that have a lasting impact in the communities they serve. By aligning the vision and strategic priorities of the school with customer-service expectations and your necessary operational procedures, you can ensure that all aspects of the operation reinforce your culture. Child care is the business of caring, compassion, kindness, and safety to educate children during the most critical years of development.

ELEMENTS OF A GREAT CULTURE

According to customer-service experts, there is just one way to provide a consistent quality experience: your culture. Jeff Toister, author of *The Service Culture Handbook*, puts it this way: "Culture creates hero moments on an individual level where employees deliver the best customer service possible. The employee feels empowered to do whatever it takes to make customers happy." As people from similar backgrounds tend to enjoy the same music, food, and art, corporate cultures are defined by the way members think, treat each other, and act. Your culture is the foundation of your recruitment strategy, the interactions among your staff and leadership, and the interactions with families and children. Teams look to managers for direction and pay attention to what leaders and directors do rather than to what they say. As a leader, your main responsibility is to provide the conditions to create a positive and caring culture. A culture that offers high-performing directors and passionate teachers a community in which they are respected and valued is one where everyone is propelled to do their best. A visitor might not know what makes the program so good, but as Colker and Koralek explain, "An engaging environment, the children's joy in learning, and the teachers' caring demeanors are signs that this programs has an intentional plan for excellence on standards of quality."

Creating a sense of culture starts with the onboarding process for new hires. It is reflected in the openness of the leadership, in the team interactions, and in the work-life balance. Beyond the professional interactions among staff and leadership, a great culture expects, encourages, and nurtures excellence.

The Onboarding Process

The onboarding process is crucial to earning a new employee's loyalty and respect. Companies that show a strong company culture from the beginning and offer trainings that are innovative, engaging, and interesting build a solid foundation. We discuss onboarding in chapter 7.

Openness for Leadership

A company needs to be unified by a common set of values, beliefs, and goals that support productivity and innovation. Management should live by those values. You can recognize openness in leadership by answering the following questions:

- Does the leadership adhere to its own corporate ideals?

- Does the leadership foster a culture of embracing change?

- Are the leaders open and willing to learn?

- Do the managers trust their employees to make decisions?

- Are people held accountable for following through on tasks?

- Can employees reach out to the director and administrative staff members?

- Can employees contact the CEO and owners directly?

Team Interactions

In a good organizational culture, teammates value collaboration and understand how to work well together. They listen to the ideas of others and value each other's ideas and opinions. They relate on an interpersonal level. Team members follow procedures most of the time, because they respect each other and understand the value of cooperation.

They function well as a team, engaging in a free exchange of dialogue and unique perspectives. Their communication is clear, transparent, and honest, from the top down and among team members.

Work-Life Balance

Management encourages a healthy work-life balance for its employees by promoting healthy habits such as exercise and eating healthy foods, encouraging efficient—not harder or more—effort, and setting an example by valuing time with their own families. Supervisors respect a regular work schedule, rather than expecting staff to routinely work overtime.

Expectations of Excellence

The process of crafting a culture of success starts with the owner and director of the school. As the evangelists of the school, the team sets the expectations not by what they say but by the way they work, communicate, and interact with customers and employees. Leadership clearly communicates goals and sets employees up for success.

Laying the foundation of a high-quality program begins by intentionally crafting a positive culture. Author of *Creating Cultures of Thinking* Ron Ritchhart looks at how culture is foundational and the hidden tool for transforming schools and offering students the best learning possible. Shapers of the culture include:

- Everyone in the group has a high interest, brought on by a sense of passion and meaning.

- Everyone is learning together and creating something greater than what one individual might produce.

- Everyone's input is valued, creating a sense of respect.

- Everyone in the group, not just the leader, uses a shared language for talking about ideas.

- Group members use open communication and engage in active listening.

- Individuals feel safe to make mistakes and take risks.

- Everyone in the group is propelled to do their best.

As a leader, your main responsibility is to provide the conditions to create a positive and caring culture. The culture starts at the top and is perpetuated by a desire to create the conditions where directors and teachers could thrive as they create a community that makes a difference in the world.

CREATING AN ENVIRONMENT WHERE A POSITIVE CULTURE CAN FLOURISH

From rowing teams, we learn the importance of working toward one vision or common goal. In the sport of rowing, everyone is held accountable for her or his performance, and team members are expected to use their oars in sync to generate speed. Similarly, once you create the conditions where members of a child-care center can work together toward common goals, you will create the best environment to support children's learning.

How do you create the environment? Author Jacob Morgan describes the attributes that set the stage to create a "celebrated" culture.

Company Is Viewed Positively

Everyone Feels Valued

Legitimate Sense of Purpose

Employees Feel Like They're Part of a Team

Believes in Diversity and Inclusion

Referrals Come from Emplyoees

Ability to Learn New Things and Given Resources to Do So and Advance

Treats Employees Fairly

Executives and Managers Are Coaches and Mentors

Dedicated to Employee Health and Wellness

Employees' perception about the company has an impact on the entire organization and how prospective employees perceive your employer branding. Employees who feel valued, are recognized for the work they do, and are offered a legitimate sense of purpose create a celebrated culture. In developing a culture of excellence, think about the following.

Step 1: Find Your Why

A strong mission is the beginning of the difference between high- and low-quality programs. I started college thinking that I would go to medical school. I once attended a class in which the professor started talking about the purpose of doctors and asked the class to complete a questionnaire about the reasons we joined the program. By the end of the class, I had disenrolled from the pre-med program. His simple questions helped me realized that medicine was not my calling. Just like medicine, child care is a mission-driven business in which people accept a big responsibility that should not be taken lightly. Educating children during the most critical years of brain development begins with self-awareness of the character traits, purpose, and mission of the child-care owner.

Write down your mission, your values, and what drives you to start the journey. It is never too late to find your path, begin an improvement process in your center, or find renewed energy for your child-care business. The secrets of running a high-quality child-care center lie within you, and the process begins with a personal commitment to accept the responsibility of shaping the lives of the next generation.

Step 2: Create Your Professional-Development Plan

Invest time in learning about the components of a high-quality program and creating your professional-development plan. To earn the license to open a child-care center, states require health and safety inspections. The next level is to start an accreditation program to ensure that certain quality standards have been met. The accreditation process is a rigorous and transformative quality-improvement system that begins with a self-study and initial questionnaire that can help owners understand what they need to do to run a high-quality center. Unfortunately, notes John Surr, author of "Who's Accredited? What and How the States Are Doing on Best Practices in Child Care," only a fraction of child-care programs in the United States pursue accreditation, as it is not a state requirement to open and operate a center. Yet, there are numerous benefits of pursuing an accreditation, including ensuring that the program incorporates high-quality standards. Accreditations allow programs to identify areas of opportunity to create processes, policies, and procedures to improve their services.

NAEYC and other accreditation agencies identify key components of high-quality programs that support and nurture healthy child development:

- **Environment:** the arrangement of space and selection of toys, materials, and equipment

- **Program structure:** the scheduling of routines and sequence of activities to promote early learning standards

- **Curriculum:** the program's offerings and experiences

- **Supportive interactions:** adult-child interactions

- **Positive guidance strategies:** teaching children self-regulation and how to manage emotions and express feelings

In addition to these components, high-quality programs offer individualized learning experiences and engage in practices that support early brain development. They encourage family engagement as a key component of a high-quality learning environment.

Child-care programs that focus on providing the best for children and families—and are not centered around financial gain—offer an environment that provides a sense of purpose and value to employees. Laying the foundation of a high-quality program begins by intentionally planning the employee experience.

Step 3: Infuse Your Vision and Mission in Every Department

Create strategies to infuse your vision and mission in every department of your organization.

Sharing your vision is part of your director's onboarding training. Let's take another look at the vision chart from pages 27-28, with ideas for infusing the culture you envision.

DEPARTMENT	STRATEGIC GOAL	VISION	INFUSE CULTURE
Sales	Have a waiting list in the first year	Our center will be operating at full capacity, and we will have a waiting list.	Offer an incentive based on service standards.
Marketing	Become the market leader in the community	We will be the market leader, and families will be our advocates in the community.	Create a parent-advocate program at the school to serve as an advisory board.
Licensing	Have a perfect licensing record	We will have an outstanding reputation in the community for perfect kindergarten-readiness scores and a perfect licensing record.	Share stories of success. For example, post in your newsletter your commitment to procedures, your licensing report, or renewal of teacher certifications.
Finance	Achieve profitability and efficiency; invest in what we value	We will operate efficiently, have increased our cash reserves for emergencies, and achieve our ROI for investors.	Create a wish list for the center. For example, if teachers want new playground equipment, have the administrative team gather estimates and then set financial goals.
Human Resources	Be considered the best place to work	Our turnover rate will be less than 20 percent this year.	Share employee stories and how they feel about the company.
Customer Service and Retention	Have high customer satisfaction and excellent customer-services experiences	Customers will be our advocates.	Have families share their experiences on social media with other families and recommend our company.
Operations	Have an outstanding reputation in the community	• Our classroom management scores will be consistently over 90 percent. • Classroom inspections and safety procedures will be followed at all times. • We will start the accreditation process.	Create an incentive program that ties to consistent implementation of procedures and accreditation standards based on scores per classrooms. The process is able to transfer accountability from the director to the teachers in the classroom.

Salesforce, a widely used customer relationship platform, has developed a free online tool to help organizations align their visions and mission. The tool is called V2MOM, which stands for:

▣ **Vision:** what you want to achieve

▣ **Values:** beliefs that help you pursue the vision

▣ **Method:** actions to get the job done

- ▣ **Obstacles:** challenges you have to overcome to achieve the vision

- ▣ **Measures:** results you aim to achieve

To learn more, see https://trailhead.salesforce.com/en/content/learn/modules/manage_the_sfdc_organizational_alignment_v2mom/msfw_oav2m_creating_org_alignment_v2mom

REBUILDING YOUR CULTURE AFTER COVID-19

You may be thinking, "This all sounds great, but we've been struggling since the beginning of the pandemic. How can we develop our culture in this challenging environment?" COVID-19 profoundly affected most child-care businesses. It forced a reduction in the workforce, closed many centers, and left the ones that remained open with fear and uncertainty. Child-care owners and directors who built cultures around compassion and empathy had to face a new reality: to protect the financial performance of the company in this economic uncertainty, they have had to reduce work hours, furlough employees, and break up teams.

Those decisions have deeply affected the culture of many organizations. For example, Erin Griffith of *The New York Times* reported that, in the midst of the pandemic, Airbnb's CEO Brian Chesky addressed thousands of his employees via webcam to announce that the company would have to cut divisions and lay off workers. These measures put Airbnb in the center of a growing debate around what happens when a company that has positioned itself as family to its employees has to choose between who should stay and who should leave. Many child-care owners have had to make difficult decisions to navigate the uncertainties of the market and now are faced with finding their way back to reestablishing the culture of their organizations.

For lessons on recovering from deep loss and upheaval, let's dive into the story of Reggio Emilia, Italy, a region in the northern part of the country. As Emily Chertoff relates in her article "Reggio Emilia: From Postwar Italy to NYC's Toniest Preschools," after World War II, the little town of Villa Cella lay in ruins. There were no jobs, no institutions or government, no schools or universities, no banks, no newspapers, and no shops. Five days after the end of the war, Chertoff relates, a rumor started circulating. A group of women had started to build a school. A young teacher in his twenties, Loris Malaguzzi, heard the rumor and jumped on his bicycle to go see it with his own eyes. When he asked the women what they were doing, they told him that they were building a school because they wanted to shelter the children from the circumstances and engage them in learning. Contrary to the common misconception, the mothers of Reggio believed their children were just as intelligent as the rich people's children and deserved a good education. Mr. Malaguzzi responded, "I'll learn as we go along and the children will learn everything I learn working with them."

The townspeople contributed whatever they could to gather enough money to keep the school running. The mothers wanted to shelter the children from the difficulties of their environment and to make sure that the teachers shared that same vision for their children. In time, the region established the first municipal preschools, and Loris Malaguzzi became the leader of a movement. Today, tourists travel to Reggio Emilia to learn the story of resilience that started one of the best early childhood education programs in the world.

This inspiring story serves as a tactical action plan for overcoming adversity after COVID-19.

Young children have the ability to create whatever they can imagine. To succeed, they need an environment to nurture them and the commitment of the adults to build a culture of respect around joy of learning, compassion, love, and respect. In the aftermath of the war, families were struggling with unemployment, uncertainty, and a devastated country. But they persevered and built the framework where their children could flourish. Like them, our present conditions do not have to define the future of the next generation. The creativity, innovation, and collaboration that is innate in young children will help them design the world they deserve.

BUILD YOUR KNOWLEDGE

Complete your own V2MOM online, or simply create a chart outlining your goals, vision, steps to take to achieve your vision, obstacles that may stand in the way, and ideas for overcoming those obstacles.

4
RECRUITING YOUR DIRECTOR

_ 66 _____

One bad apple spoils the whole barrel.

—PROVERB

MAIN QUESTIONS

» What is the ideal profile of a child-care director?

» What are the biggest operational challenges directors face?

» What are the challenges of a dual-management system in child care?

» What are good interview questions to help owners recruit directors?

» What are the strategies to communicate the mission of a school?

» What is the difference between a manager and a leader?

» What is the biggest contributor to employee engagement?

360-degree evaluation: a process in which employees receive confidential, anonymous feedback from the people who work around them, such as the employee's manager, peers, and direct reports

Employee referral program: a program that rewards or offers bonuses to employees who find new employees

Ideal target customer: type of person you want to market to, based on demographic information and an understanding of customer needs

Sell sheet: a one-page document that details the features of a product or service

Social listening: the practice of monitoring digital conversations to understand what customers are saying about a brand and industry online; a tool to help differentiate a brand, product, or service from the competition

Case Study: A Bad Experience Leads to a New Tool

I tend to look for positive qualities in everyone. I used to think everyone could grow into a position. Yet, one of my worst hiring decisions revealed that I had to stop trusting my instincts, create a process, and make a collaborative recruiting effort. Owners have to identify early on when a candidate is not a right fit, ask others for opinions, and carefully observe any warning signs. One of the worst things that can happen for a new school is to recruit the wrong person for the director's position and have to let her go in a short period of time.

I decided to hire a candidate for a chief operating officer (COO) position who met the experience and education requirements to oversee a group of directors. She had been a director, had worked at an early learning coalition, and seemed really nice. She was constantly praising me as a strategy to become my trusted advisor. But that was just with me. The moment she was not around me, her authoritative style emerged. She was vengeful if someone challenged her, loved playing the team against each other, lacked any empathy for teachers, and was unkind. She was the kind of manager who says, "You do this because I say so." She was motivated by power, had a need for revenge for being laid off from her previous position, and thought every staff member was replaceable—except her. Her approach was very different from our vision and leadership style.

Looking back, I did see some warning signs, but I intentionally ignored them. For example, she criticized her previous boss during the job interview and overplayed her achievements. But I ignored the signs and followed the standard recruiting practices, such as calling references.

In a short period of time, we started to witness how our team had been affected by this one bad hiring decision. Directors stopped giving suggestions and started fighting instead of collaborating with each other. Gossip circulated in the company, good employees were unhappy, and turnover was out of control.

Luckily, I had built trust with my team, and they knew they could come to me to share their concerns about the new COO. Ultimately, dealing with the problem was my responsibility, as I had failed to include trusted directors and staff members in the hiring process.

Yes, one bad apple can spoil the entire bunch. The longer you keep a bad recruit, the more negativity will spread, especially if that recruit is in a leadership position. Almost anyone can temporarily appear to fit the requirements of a job and the culture of a company, but character and competency are tested over time. Therefore, you need a process that holds a person accountable for expectations and considers information from the person's direct reports. Recruiting the right candidate is not a decision—it is a process, for both directors and owners.

Thanks to this bad hiring experience, we asked a recruiter to help design a process for the child-care industry that we informally call the "matchmaking strategy" for owners and directors.

Recruiter Mechy Avalos, who was also one of our parents, invited teachers, directors, and families to participate in sessions to help her identify the characteristics of an ideal child-care director and COO. If we could craft scenarios and create questions that would help us dive deeper into internal motivations to create potential scenarios, that information would help us identify warning signs during the interview process. As part of the design process, we wrote down the profile of a non-ideal candidate. We described the character traits of the person I had regrettably hired: constant praise to a boss, lack of empathy for others, motivated by power, contentious, arrogant, and authoritative. We also created the same type of profile for non-ideal teachers.

THE DUAL-MANAGEMENT SYSTEM

One of the challenges of the dual-management system in the child-care industry is that each side of the organization has different priorities. Therefore, alignment and clear communication are critical. To understand the priorities of both sides of an organization, I sent a survey to a group of owners and directors. The owners I surveyed said that their priorities were recouping their investments, reaching or improving profitability, and increasing enrollment. Directors had very different priorities: recruiting and retaining teachers, addressing customer-service issues, complying with licensing authorities, marketing, and maintaining scores and enrollment.

HiMama's 2019 North American benchmark report illustrates that the biggest operational risk for directors is keeping both customers and employees happy. A healthy alignment between the owner and the director is critical in setting the foundation for developing a quality-centered business plan and building a strong team. The relationship between the owner and director will dictate the culture of the organization.

Just like dating someone a few times, there is no guarantee that a job candidate will be a good fit until you have actually gone through different experiences with the person. High-performing directors tend to choose work environments where they can thrive and grow. Mrs. Mary, a preschool teacher at my first school, offers a great example to illustrate this principle. From the moment I met her, I was confident that she had so much potential to become a director. Sure enough, in a few years, she accomplished this goal.

One of her biggest challenges as a director was the pressing need to repair the playground equipment. In discussing her challenges with the absentee owner, the owner explained that the facility lacked the resources to pay for the repairs. Mary explained to the owner that she had already received a violation for the condition of the playground, yet she was left to figure out how to replace broken toys, repair the playground equipment, and improve the physical environment to stay in compliance. She asked for donations, recruited a group of teacher volunteers to paint the facility on the weekends, and conducted a fundraising campaign to repair the playground. Although she succeeded in making the necessary repairs to the playground, she couldn't understand why the school had been unable to afford those expenses. After all, she had just enrolled ten new families, and the owner would not give her a valid explanation. Mary started looking for a new job. The reality is that good employees don't leave companies. They leave their bosses.

Matching an ideal owner with an ideal director is a two-way process. Therefore, this chapter includes tips for both directors and owners. Recruiting requires you to have not only leadership skills but also some business acumen or understanding of child-care operations.

DEVELOPING A RECRUITING STRATEGY TO FIND THE RIGHT DIRECTOR

The process starts by understanding what you need to offer as a company and whom you are trying to recruit. Recruiting for the director position takes time. You will need a carefully crafted action plan to attract the candidates you are looking for. Attracting the attention of directors is especially challenging, as you are most likely trying to recruit directors with experience working for competitors or who are moving into your area.

Step 1: Create a Profile of Your Ideal Candidate

Creating an ideal persona is a method practiced by marketing teams to identify patterns and common characteristics of the customers they most want to reach. You can use a similar technique to develop an ideal candidate persona, which will give you a clearer understanding of who might be the right cultural fit for your company. Also invest some time in creating negative personas—the candidates whom you wouldn't consider hiring. This process takes research and planning, as it requires you to consider the different perspectives of candidates, customers, employees, and management, but it is worth the time and effort.

From the candidates' perspective, think about questions such as, "What problems could they be facing?" "What are their goals likely to be?" "Why would they want to quit their current jobs?" To learn answers to your questions, practice social listening; join professional organizations, such as the NAEYC, the Division for Early Childhood (DEC) of the Council for Exceptional Children, and Zero to Three; and attend local events for directors. Your research will reveal patterns and common characteristics for directors, as well as their challenges, goals, and motivations.

Start by building the profile of a director whom you know and respect. In the profile, include information and answers to four main questions: who, what, why, and how. As an example, I am using a profile of my friend and colleague, Misti Castner.

Who?

> » *Name: Misti Castner*

> » *Current title: Early Childhood Director, ABC Child Care*

> » *Time in current position: has worked at ABC for 15 years; director for 5 years*

> » *Position applying for: Early Childhood Director, My Child Care*

> » *Education: Bachelor of Science, Early Childhood Development, Notareal University, Anytown, USA*

> » *Current location: Orlando, FL*

> » *Communication preferences: email (mcastner@notarealemail.com)*

Next, list the candidate's goals and challenges. Then list some ways that your company could help the candidate achieve her goals and handle her challenges.

What?

> » *Misti's goals: professional development*

> » *Misti's challenges:*

>> ≳ *the unknowns of the current child-care market*
>> ≳ *meeting financial goals*
>> ≳ *furloughing employees*

> » *Our solutions for her:*

>> ≳ *Training or seminars on leadership and communication*
>> ≳ *A healthy, stress-free environment*
>> ≳ *Positive guidance and reassurance*
>> ≳ *Support and creative strategies to bring in new families*

Think about the reasons why the candidate might want to work for your company. Then think about why she might *not* want to work for you.

Why?

> » *Why are her goals important to Misti? Professional development will enhance her growth and performance as an administrator and will enhance her connections with families and staff.*

> » *What are her concerns about her current company? She struggles with sudden changes in focus and with the personal sacrifices needed to meet the high demands of her ever-shifting job description during COVID-19.*

> » *Why wouldn't she want to work for us?*

⋛ *Stress and the unknowns of a new company*
⋛ *Instability as she makes a transition*

Finally, consider the candidate's values, accomplishments, challenges, and inspiration. You will use these details to craft an effective message in a way that will be most appealing to her. What is your elevator pitch? How will you describe your company to her?

How?

» *What does your director value?*

» *What are her biggest accomplishments? challenges?*

» *What inspires her?*

Step 2: Develop a Recruitment Strategy

Attracting the attention of targeted individuals is difficult because they might be working for a competitor or they may be passive job seekers. Therefore, pay attention to your branding recruitment messages, networking strategy, and culture.

Before recruiting for the position, determine the requirements of the job to effectively delegate the responsibilities. Traditional job descriptions list activities in specific categories that can help you create your job description.

Once you have determined the job requirements for the position and created a profile of the ideal candidate for the director position, you are ready for the next step of the process: developing a recruitment strategy, a formal plan to recruit the best talent to fill the position. Tips to recruit directors include the following:

- ⊡ **Create a sell sheet.** The starting point of a recruiting strategy is to understand your selling points as an employer. Determine your compensation and benefits (such as vacation days) before listing the intangibles of working for your company. You could list, for example, a great culture, empowerment, the philosophy of your program, and your mission. Your sell sheet explains why candidates would want to come to work at your school and is important in helping you craft a recruiting message.

- ⊡ **Research the main challenges directors face.** Another important strategy is to understand the main challenges that directors face in your community. During the interview, offer solutions and start building bridges of understanding with the candidate. For example, if directors in the community are struggling to recruit certified teachers, consider offering a solution such as allocating a training budget to develop teachers.

- **Establish relationships with local community colleges and high schools.** Educational programs that train teachers or offer child-development associate (CDA) training are good places to find ideal candidates.

- **Join professional organizations**. Use what you learn to understand patterns and common characteristics for directors, as well as their challenges, goals, and motivations.

- **Connect with prospective employees** via LinkedIn or other social media. Companies have begun experimenting with recruitment strategies on social media with sponsored stories, using professional sites such as LinkedIn to offer the job opening to targeted individuals. This is becoming increasingly important as candidates follow potential employers on social media to learn about job openings and the employer's culture. According to an article by Tressa Richards for Rally Recruitment, a Glassdoor study revealed that 79 percent of candidates use social media when searching for their next opportunity, and according to LinkedIn research, almost 50 percent of them follow potential employers on social sites to stay aware of available roles. Microsoft, for example, uses social platforms to highlight employee stories. By highlighting a new team member or providing a glimpse of what it is like to work at the company, Microsoft connects with its ideal candidate on a consistent basis.

- **Create a careers page on your website.** According to a 2020 article on Betterteam.com about common recruitment strategy mistakes, experts suggest treating your recruitment strategy as a sales funnel by having powerful recruitment branding. One way to promote your brand is to create a careers page on your website where anyone who visits the page learns about your school. Job seekers, in particular, want to understand your mission, your values, and what you consider important. This page would also list the requirements for the job you are recruiting for.

- **Seek referrals.** Employee or family referral is one of the most powerful and commonly used methods as a source for finding potential job candidates. Referrals of prospective candidates bring attention to your job opening and get the attention of directors who might not be actively looking for a job. For start-up schools, networking in your community through community colleges, directors' networks, and government agencies might provide a great source of candidates. You can also get referrals from companies with whom you have a business relationship. When companies value and respect your reputation, they will be willing to refer candidates. For existing schools or expansions, an employee referral program that offers bonuses to employees for successful referrals is an economical recruitment method.

Step 3: Conduct Prescreening

Consider creating a recruiting team, such as a panel or an interview team, to participate in this step of the process. To save time for the team, contact each candidate to determine the candidate's credentials and salary expectations. Review the information you have on the applicants for the position, and select those who meet the technical requirements for the job: number of years in their current position, minimum level of education, and technical skill and certifications for the job.

Step 4: Conduct Face-to-Face Interviews with the Candidates

Invite each candidate for an initial interview, either in person or virtually. This first interview should be short (thirty minutes) so you can decide not only whether the candidate meets the qualifications of the job but also whether she would be a good candidate for a more in-depth interview. Encourage candidates to ask questions as well. Preparing interview questions beforehand will help you determine whether the candidate meets the requirements for the job and is a good cultural fit for your company. The following are some sample questions to choose from.

Technical skills for the job:

- ▣ Tell me about yourself.

- ▣ What early childhood philosophy do you practice?

- ▣ Tell me something that changed your perspective in early childhood, either positively or negatively.

- ▣ Have you tried to get a program accredited? Have you received licensing violations in the past year?

Leadership questions:

- ▣ In the past, what have been your biggest challenges in building a team?

- ▣ What are the characteristics of a negative culture?

- Tell me about a team you have developed. Which strategies did you use?

- How do you handle gossip in the workplace? Why do you think it happens?

- How is the retention with your staff?

- How is your turnover?

- Tell me about a challenging situation you faced as a leader.

- Tell me about your employer. (Note: If the candidate speaks negatively about her employer, that is a warning sign.)

- What would your staff say about you?

- Give me an example of a time you facilitated change in your current school. What was the impact of the change, and what did you learn from the process?

- How have you motivated your school to embrace a new initiative, such as an accreditation? What impact did the initiative have?

- Tell me about someone you have mentored.

- How do you effectively motivate, develop, and direct your staff?

Management questions:

- How many staff members do you have in your team?

- How do you supervise teachers to make sure they follow procedures?

- How do you evaluate the productivity of your staff?

- How do you ensure that staff members are held accountable for their performance?

- How do you stay current on children's activities and teaching techniques?

- How do you set up priorities?

- Talk me through how you manage your workload. How do you manage the unexpected?

- How do you organize, plan, and prioritize your work?

- How did you manage the COVID-19 crisis at your center? What challenges did you face?

Customer-service questions:

- Describe a time when you dealt with an unhappy parent. How did you resolve the matter?

- How do you keep self-composure when a customer is emotional?

- What other incentives have you implemented at your previous job to reward customers?

Financial management questions:

- Are you involved with the financial aspect of your operation?

- If yes: In what ways?

- If no: Who handles the financial aspect of your operation?

Sales and marketing questions:

- Tell me about your enrollment. Did you meet your goals?

- In your previous/current job, what percentage of tours did you close?

If you are satisfied with a candidate's responses to your questions in the initial interview, schedule a second, more in-depth interview. Ask questions such as the following.

Questions to reveal whether the candidate has a growth mindset:

- Tell me about something you want to learn that is difficult.

- Give me an example of when you accomplished a personally challenging goal.

- Do you have a coach? Who would you consider your mentor in the field?

- Who is your go-to person when you face a challenging situation in the industry?

- Tell me about a time you failed and how you overcame it.

- How do you help your team reach its full potential?

- Describe a time when your ethics were challenged.

- How do you handle stressful situations?

Questions to reveal the candidate's long-term goals:

- ▣ What are your professional goals for the next five years?

- ▣ What are your professional-development goals?

- ▣ Share an example of when you went above and beyond the call of duty.

- ▣ Why are you looking to leave your current job?

- ▣ Why are you the best candidate for this position?

The conversation should, of course, be two-way. As an interviewer, be prepared to answer questions such as the following:

- ▣ Why did you choose the child-care industry?

- ▣ Who are your main competitors?

- ▣ What makes your program different?

- ▣ What is the mission of your program?

- ▣ Who is your ideal customer?

- ▣ What are your expectations for the position I'm interviewing for?

- ▣ What is your vision?

- ▣ What is the educational philosophy of your company?

- ▣ What are your main organizational priorities?

- ▣ What are your long-term goals? Do you want to open other centers? expand?

- ▣ What do you understand will be the main operational challenges?

- ▣ How will you support the director?

Step 5: Ask the Candidate to Complete a Personality and Leadership Assessment

Assessments are tools that organizations can use in the hiring process. There are many different types of pre-employment tests that measure qualities, job fit and skills, and job readiness. Some job boards include assessments that candidates should complete before the interview.

Results from your candidate's personality assessment, leadership style, and emotional-intelligence test can help you understand whether the candidate is a good cultural fit for your team.

To find out what you are looking for, you might need to dive deeper into the qualities of the negative profile of the candidate. Understanding what you are not looking for can help you create a list of questions. For example, if you are trying to hire someone who is humble, you might include a question about a mistake she has made. The type of response will reveal some of the candidate's character traits. In this case, an arrogant person will talk too much about her merit and probably says she knows everything or hasn't made mistakes. A humble person will be open to discussing the mistake and lessons learned.

Another scenario is asking a question about how the candidate has helped others. This could play out in two ways. A person who lacks empathy will not be able to talk about an example of helping others without including a description that makes herself look like a hero. A person with empathy will most likely play a secondary role in the description.

The following are a few sample questions:

- Tell me about something you have done wrong in your job, or tell me about a time you failed professionally. What did you learn from the experience?

- What is something that you would like to learn to do your job better?

- Tell me about something you have done to improve the working conditions of early childhood education professionals.

Step 6: Immerse the Candidate in Experiences

From the human-resources world, we can learn great tips that we can incorporate into our recruiting practices. These activities will give you insight into how a candidate might handle challenging situations that can occur in early childhood programs.

The inbox activity:

A useful activity includes business simulations of what the director could find in her inbox. These simulations allow the recruiter to see how the candidate will prioritize and handle the unexpected. For example, offer one of the following challenges, and ask the candidate to describe how she would respond.

- A parent account shows that the family owes $2,000.

- The air conditioning in one of the classrooms is not working.

- Your infant teacher called in sick, and you have to find someone to cover for her.

- The infant-room teacher came in to complain about her assistant's performance.

The school tour:

Before opening the school, intentionally go around the school to prepare for this activity. Create some scenarios that would be considered violations should an inspector arrive, such as misplaced medication or a cleaning product left out where a child could reach it. You can use your state's licensing record to create the scenarios. Conduct a school tour with the candidate. It is a great sign if the person identifies the situations during your walkthrough.

Step 7: Complete a Rubric to Keep Track of Your Candidates

Keep an organized list of candidates, and take notes on responses to interview questions. Develop a process to follow up, such as connecting with them to explain the process or answer any questions. As best practice, I recommend treating your candidates the same way you treat a parent. Through the interview process, you are defining your recruitment expectations for your entire organization.

Upon completion of the interviews, complete a rubric and review your notes. Some candidates will no longer be under consideration immediately; typically, that will be obvious by their low scores. The candidates with the highest scores will continue in the next step of the process: reference and background check. You can create your own rubric and weight the items as you see fit. Here's one to use as an example.

CANDIDATE	HELEN WILLIAMS	MARK SELLARS	TENESHIA JONES	LUPE VASQUEZ
Technical Requirements	10	10	10	9
Education Requirements	10	10	10	10
Background Checks and References	8	9	10	9
Personality and Leadership Assessment	6	7	8	10
School Inspection	6	8	10	8
HR Scenarios	8	6	7	7
Cultural Fit	10	8	9	8

Step 8: Ask the Candidates You've Selected for Their References, and Verify Their Education and Licensing Records

The job references provided by the candidates are the names and contact information of individuals who can attest to their abilities. Ask for references from the candidates' places of employment, families from the schools where they have been a director, and coworkers. In addition to contacting references, look at each candidate's current center website and at online and social-media sites, such as Glassdoor and Facebook. Verify that the candidate has successfully completed the required education, and check licensing records at her previous job. Directors who are detailed oriented pay close attention to their licensing records.

I once interviewed a candidate for a director position who had great references and a perfect licensing record. After several interviews, I decided to check Glassdoor and Facebook reviews of her former school, which revealed that she did not fit our culture. She had received too many bad reviews related to customer service from her previous employees.

Step 9: Take Each Final Candidate on a Lunch Interview

Meet each candidate in a nonwork environment so you can dive deeper into shared values. In this interview, you might be able to identify some warning signs. After the interview, complete the rubric to help you make your selection.

As described in the article "The 'Innerview': A Tool for Employee Engagement" by Terry Siebert, the Dale Carnegie training company developed a tool called the *Innerview* to unveil the inner motivations of candidates. The company suggests that, by deepening a leader's connection with a prospective candidate in a casual conversation, the leader can discover shared values. The tool is divided into three parts: factual questions, causative questions, and value-driven questions. I recommend both the interviewer and the interviewee ask the same questions. You can use the following questions as conversation prompts during the interview.

Factual questions:

- Where did you grow up?

- What were your interests in school?

- What do you do for fun?

- What early childhood philosophy do you practice?

- What is your view on discipline?

Causative questions:

- ☑ Why did you study early childhood education?

- ☑ Why did you pick that particular school?

- ☑ What brought you to your current job?

- ☑ What direction did you go in right after high school?

- ☑ What do you enjoy most about being a director?

- ☑ What do you like most about your job? What do you like least?

- ☑ Why did you enter the industry?

- ☑ What keeps you going every day?

- ☑ What did you learn about yourself during the COVID-19 crisis?

Value-driven questions:

- ☑ Tell me about a person who had a major impact on your life.

- ☑ If you had to do your career all over again what, if anything, would you do differently?

- ☑ If there were a major turning point in your professional life, what might that be?

- ☑ There are many highs and lows as you go through life. Are there any of either that had a significant influence on you?

- ☑ What words of wisdom would you give a young person if he or she sought your advice?

- ☑ How would you sum up your personal philosophy in a sentence or two?

- ☑ Can you think of a time when you lost your temper? What did you learn from it?

- ☑ What would you say is your ultimate failure? What did you learn from it?

- ☑ Tell me about a time when you had to deal with conflict.

- ☑ What do you want to learn more about?

Step 10: Make Your Selection and Extend the Offer

Ideally, you want to hire someone who has the skills and is a perfect fit for the culture you want to create, but sometimes that is not possible. For example, a skilled director with a perfect licensing record might not be the best cultural fit for your organization. During the initial onboarding phase, you will have the opportunity to work closely with the director, model the expected behaviors, and shape the culture of your organization.

Send an offer letter with the basic information about the job title, supervisor, base pay, benefits, and any terms and conditions for the employment. For the candidates not selected, notify them via email, as they might be good fit for another site or a possible position with your school at another time.

According to "A Window on Early Childhood Administrative Practices," an executive summary published by the McCormick Center for Early Childhood Leadership, research identifies that administrative practices are crucial for ensuring high-quality outcomes for children and families. Therefore, recruiting, investing in professional development, and retaining the right director is critical for your child-care organization. The employees' recruiting experiences define your company culture. Owners create the director's employee experience, and that sets the tone and establishes your expectations for all other employee experiences. We will take a closer look at creating the employee experience in chapter 7.

I have had the privilege to work closely with high-performing directors to understand their mindset. They understand that their primary responsibility is to teach adults how to respect children's creative confidence and advocate for their rights. They inspire teaching teams, families, and their communities. They bring communities together because they can see beyond their job description. They build legacies that transform our society. High-performing directors can see that inside every child there is an adult who is going to change the world. They keep their core beliefs and values intact, and everything else falls into place. I'd like to give special recognition to the high-performing directors in my life. Thanks for making this world a better place.

BUILD YOUR KNOWLEDGE

» What are the main challenges directors face?

» What are the skills required to perform the job of a director?

» What is the biggest contributor to employee engagement?

» What is the difference between a manager and a leader?

» Can you think of specific tasks that directors perform as managers?

» Can you think of specific skills that directors need to become leaders?

» What are strategies to motivate a high-performing director?

Create an ideal director persona and a non-ideal director persona.

5
THE DIRECTOR'S ONBOARDING EXPERIENCE

_⟨⟨_____

*Presenting leadership as a list of carefully defined qualities
(like strategic, analytical, and performance-oriented)
no longer holds. Instead, true leadership stems from
individuality that is honestly and sometimes imperfectly
expressed. Leaders should strive for authenticity over
perfection.*

— SHERYL SANDBERG, COO, FACEBOOK

MAIN QUESTIONS

» What are the director's biggest challenges?

» Can we train happy teachers to become confident leaders?

» What are some of the personal characteristics of high-performing directors?

» How can you make policy-and-procedure training hands-on?

» Why is it important to plan the onboarding experience for the director?

» What aspects of your program require more orientation?

» What is the difference between leadership and management?

» What is the best way to introduce the director's job description?

» What is the best way to transfer accountability?

» How do you create a director's operations dashboard?

TERMS TO KNOW

Customer satisfaction score (CSAT): This metric measures how happy your customers are.

Net promoter score (NPS): Similar to CSAT, a metric that calculates how likely a customer is to recommend your company or product

SMART goals: specific, measurable, assignable, relevant, and time-bound objectives

SWOT analysis: SWOT stands for strengths, weaknesses, opportunities, and threats. Understanding your SWOT analysis helps identify your top strengths and marketing differentiators and compare them to those of your competitors. (Discussed in depth in the first book in this series, *The Basics of Starting a Child-Care Business.*)

Case Study: A Busy Morning

Jordan started her day by greeting children and their families at the door. One of her families requested to meet with her with the intention of telling her that a relative from out of town was going to pick up their child. Another parent approached her with a concern about a rash. Before she could write a note, the phone rang. It was the infant-room teacher telling Jordan that the teacher's assistant was late and she needed extra help. The director started calling other classrooms to find another teacher. She dealt with all this while standing at the reception desk with a big smile on her face.

Directors work in a fast-paced environment that leaves no room for boredom. In a director's world, every day is a new adventure, a new drama, or just putting a stop to new gossip. I served for many years as a director, and most days I felt like a cast member in a reality show. For a rookie director to become a black-belt professional, she has to be allowed to grow at her own professional pace. Like children, each one of us develops and blossoms in our own timing. No matter what stage of their career they are in, directors need an environment of trust and empowerment that allows a certain amount of failure.

As Laura Colker and Derry Koralek describe in *High-Quality Early Childhood Programs*, successful directors make everything seem easy. They are strategic, confident, and prepared to handle emergencies. They build cultures centered on compassion, discipline, competence, and performance. High-quality standards are evident in every aspect of the operation. The moment you walk inside their schools, you start experiencing the difference. Employees, families, and teachers are happy and engaged. There is abundant evidence in the center of children's learning, activities, family engagement, and health and safety protocols.

On the opposite side are directors who barely make it through the day. They struggle to find files and hide from parents demanding explanations. They might work many hours but still are not able to finish the work. They are cited for violations from licensing representatives. Their staff is not engaged, and gossip circulates around the school. They resist change, do not execute, and run from emergency to emergency the entire day.

We asked a group of directors in our community to participate in a survey that would help us understand the challenges directors face in different child-care settings. Regardless of the size of the school, directors say they are challenged by the following:

1. Maintaining health and safety

2. Recruiting passionate teachers who will work for low wages

3. Collecting parent fees and dealing with billing issues

4. Handling customer-service issues

5. Staying ahead of new competitors

The director's job requires training and many different skills. According to 2018 data published by the McCormick Center for Early Childhood Leadership, there are almost 62,000 early childhood directors in the United States (Abel, Talan, and Magid, 2018). Based on the findings and recommendations of the report, there is a pressing need for program administrators to receive specialized training, including leadership training. Further, the report suggests that many directors will benefit from additional training, regardless of their credential status.

Child-care operations entail human-resources management, compliance with policies, hiring, facilities management and maintenance, curriculum implementation, adherence to safety procedures, sales and marketing, and so many other areas. According to *State of the American Manager*, a paper published by Gallup, research shows that a manager accounts for at least 70 percent of employee engagement scores across all industries. Thus, if we develop good managers, staff members will be engaged. Gallup also states that a staggering 85 percent of employees worldwide are not engaged across all industries, which translates into most companies failing to recruit the right managers. Let's put this into perspective. Across all industries, we are promoting managers who are not a good fit for their role. The *State of the American Manager* report suggests that one of the main reasons is that companies promote managers as a reward for longevity or based on reviews or technical knowledge in a previous position.

After reading the Gallup report, I realized that we had also fallen into the trap of turning happy teachers into frustrated managers. The talents that made those teachers successful in their previous jobs were not the same skills needed to become a great manager.

BEHIND THE SCENES OF DESIGNING THE DIRECTOR'S ONBOARDING EXPERIENCE

A couple of years ago, we experienced a growth period that necessitated hiring more directors. One of our goals was to recruit talent from within, so we considered promoting teachers based on their performance reviews, industry expertise, and willingness to grow within the organization.

Once we started fast-tracking employees to management positions, we started observing unusual behaviors. One of the new directors was hiding from parents when confronted with customer-service complaints. Another was working eighteen-hours shifts but not getting the job done.

We learned from experience that the talents that made teachers successful in their previous jobs were not the same skills needed to become a great manager or a leader. We had successfully turned happy teachers into frustrated directors.

In a span of two years, our goal of recruiting talent from within had failed 50 percent of the time. All of the teachers we promoted were excited to become directors, but some did not develop all the skills to succeed at the position. Of the 50 percent who were not able to perform the director's job, 25 percent asked to go back to their previous job and 25 percent left the industry altogether.

Becoming a high-performing director takes an intentionally designed onboarding experience, mentoring, shadowing a leader, and time. You cannot fast-track the process. From our onboarding strategy, we learned that we had to develop a new process to recruit and onboard directors.

> The talents that made teachers successful in their previous jobs were not the same skills needed to become a great manager or a leader. We had successfully turned happy teachers into frustrated directors.

When they were beginning their new positions, we had asked the directors to complete a leadership self-assessment. Their scores revealed an interesting trend. The ultimately successful directors gave themselves lower scores in every category; they were eager to learn and receive mentorship. In contrast, the people who were ultimately unsuccessful as directors—the happy teachers group—scored themselves high in every category.

Some in our happy teachers group did not recognize their weaknesses and interpreted their performance review as a threat from a supervisor or as a sign of failure. Some in this group did not understand some aspects of the operations and relied constantly on their supervisor for external motivation and coaching. Others simply did not enjoy the director's position.

Directors in all groups had accepted the position because they didn't want to disappoint the manager who had recommended them. They were excited about the position when they started, but not all had developed the skills required for the job. For example, one of the participants was organized but had to improve her communication skills. Consequently, she was having problems motivating her staff members. That undeveloped skill caused the majority of her problems. Another new director was not able to transition from the role of a colleague to the role of a leader at the same location. She knew what she had to do, but she did not know how to get started.

QUALITIES OF SUCCESSFUL DIRECTORS

When my son Oliver was a preschooler, I wanted him to become a martial-arts expert. I bought him all the uniforms for his training. I remember helping him get ready for class and putting his white belt around his waist. Before practice, I motivated him with positive comments and made sure he knew some basic rules. He was not excited about the class after his first attempt, but I convinced him to try it many times until going to the martial-arts class had become torture for both of us. I was determined and persistent. There was just one problem: he was not passionate about martial arts.

In the same way my son needed internal motivation to pursue this new sport, there is no way we can turn a rookie director into a high-performing leader without internal motivation. The director's internal motivation guides her during the journey. Motivation, attitude, passion, grit, and persistence are internal resources necessary in the process of mastering any discipline.

Our "black belt" directors have had different personalities and leadership styles. Take Erika and Misti, for example. Erika is the life of the party, with a warm and bubbly personality. In contrast, Misti is more reserved and analytical. Both of them are caring, ethical, and guided by a strong set of values. Even though they are very different individuals, they have some characteristics in common:

- Self-aware and able to recognize their weaknesses, strengths, drive, and values

- Caring and empathetic

- Passionate about early childhood education

- Humble and unafraid to ask for help

- Empowered and reliable

- Resourceful

- Assertive yet kind

- Open to opportunities to improve their programs

- Motivated by intrinsic values and a strong sense of mission

- Self-controlled under difficult circumstances

- Determined and committed to their success

- Committed to a healthy work-life balance

- Highly organized and detail oriented

- Emotionally intelligent

- Have a growth mindset

- Able to build rapport and motivate staff

- Confident learners

- Unafraid of change

- Active and effective mentors

The educational level of the employee does not guarantee that she will become a great director or leader. A master's degree in educational leadership does not guarantee leadership skills. Our "black belt" directors had access to a support network of peers or a mentor. They were all managers with technical knowledge of child development, and all had started as teachers and transitioned into a leadership role. Therefore, they demonstrated high levels of empathy for new teachers, which allowed them to have credibility with the team.

Leadership Skills versus Management Skills

High-performing directors possess technical knowledge, leadership, and management skills.

According to the website Next Generation, there's a difference between a manager and a leader. Yet, the distinction between two roles often get confused. A manager focuses on people, problems, and tasks at hand using technical skills to address them. A leader translates values into actions, turns organizations into successful ventures, and prepares others for change.

Leading a child-care business involves getting people to believe the vision you set for the company and to work with you to achieve your goals. Management is about making sure the day-to-day activities get done. As managers, directors run the day-to-day operations of the facility; follow processes, procedures, requirements, rules, and regulations; and address issues with families and staff members. As leaders, directors create the environment to support the culture children need to thrive.

The director as a manager:

- is responsible for keeping records;

- complies with licensing agencies;

- maintains high standards in the facility;

- implements tactical actions;

- measures center performance;

- develops systems to ensure high standards;

- plans and organizes use of resources;

- establishes systems to oversee curriculum implementation;

- manages staff, including recruiting, hiring, training, and firing;

- assesses children's progress;

- maintains safe, clean indoor and outdoor physical environments; and

- communicates with families and encourages their involvement in their children's education.

Guiding early childhood programs with a vision requires more than management skills. Child-care directors who thrive motivate their teams, inspire them to achieve goals, and create a positive culture centered on values. These skills translate into high-performing teams and profitability.

The director as a leader:

- creates a vision and goals and aligns people,

- prepares the team for change and helps the team navigate through challenges,

- understands that excellence is a pursuit that never ends,

- identifies potential problems before they happen,

- looks for ways to improve the program and turns problems into improvement plans,

- conducts classroom observations regularly,

- creates organizational structures for record keeping,

- seeks feedback from staff and families on ways to improve performance,

- remains humble and accepts suggestions for improvement,

- develops people and establishes leadership-succession plans,

- inspires staff members,

- ☑ designs improvement plans,

- ☑ develops strategic growth plans,

- ☑ seeks third-party accreditation for her programs, and

- ☑ identifies community partnerships that can help support program goals.

"Black belt" directors in the making are self-driven, need a specific environment to succeed, have a growth mindset, and do not like to be micromanaged. They welcome a challenge, a purpose, clear goals and expectations, and the freedom to define their culture and grow at their own pace. These directors are looking not only for a job but also for a mission to fulfill their passion. Just like plants need fertile ground, high-performing directors need an environment that allows them to learn and grow. The challenge is to provide an environment that enables high-performing directors to blossom and offers opportunities for entry-level employees to discover and develop new skills.

DESIGNING THE DIRECTOR'S ONBOARDING EXPERIENCE

Corporations can create career opportunities for directors if they have systems in place to recruit, onboard, and train top performers. Yet, independent operators and franchisees sometimes lack processes to design the director's onboarding experience. According to Madeline Laurano of the Aberdeen Group, only 32 percent of employers have a formal onboarding process, despite that 54 percent of companies that offer a formal onboarding experience report significant gains in employee productivity engagement and 50 percent see greater employee retention.

According to an article on the Society for Human Resource Management (SHRM) website by Roy Maurer, 90 percent of new hires decide whether or not to stay in the company in the first six months. Maurer says that 58 percent of employees are more likely to stay in a company three years later if they have completed a structured onboarding process. A well-designed onboarding process has an effect on engagement and retention.

Start by empathizing with a new director on her first day on the job. From the employee's perspective, it's exciting to start a new job. From an owner's perspective, it's exciting to start a new business. Yet, onboarding employees is usually a torturous process for owners and directors, with piles of paperwork to sign and many manuals to read.

The initial onboarding training is a process that varies in length, taking anywhere from a few days to several months. It begins with the director's training to set the expectations for the rest of the team. The process allows the owner to set the expectations of the company and share the vision and culture of the company and the milestones of the business plan. I have designed some experiences that you can incorporate into your own onboarding process at your own pace.

Step 1: Pre-onboarding

Consider the following as you plan to get your director ready for the first day.

- **Prepare a warm welcome.** Consider sending a video, text, or voicemail to let her know how happy you are to have her on your team. Provide information on parking and an orientation checklist. Have the staff handbook, the new director's business cards, email, software, and office space ready.

- **Plan the training schedule and onboarding checklist.** The following is a sample director's checklist and training schedule that we have used in my company to set the expectations for the onboarding experience. Adapt it as needed to create your own checklist.

NEW-HIRE CHECKLIST

Employee Information

Name: _____

Position: _____

Start date: _____

Manager: _____

Provide employee with employee handbook. Review key policies:

- ☐ Anti-harassment
- ☐ Vacation and sick leave
- ☐ Family Medical Leave Act/leaves of absence
- ☐ Personal conduct standards
- ☐ Progressive disciplinary actions
- ☐ Security

- [ ] Holidays
- [ ] Time and leave reporting
- [ ] Overtime
- [ ] Payroll timing
- [ ] Performance reviews
- [ ] Dress code
- [ ] Confidentiality
- [ ] Safety
- [ ] Emergency procedures
- [ ] Visitors
- [ ] Email and internet use

Review general administrative procedures:

- [ ] Office/desk/classroom
- [ ] Keys and building access cards
- [ ] Mail and shipping
- [ ] Purchase requests
- [ ] Telephones
- [ ] Conference rooms
- [ ] Picture ID badges
- [ ] Expense reports
- [ ] Office supplies
- [ ] Computers
- [ ] Email and internet
- [ ] Data on shared drives
- [ ] Children's files

Conduct general orientation and tour:

- [ ] Playground
- [ ] Staff restrooms
- [ ] Children's restrooms
- [ ] Copy machines and printers
- [ ] Parking
- [ ] Supply closets
- [ ] Kitchen
- [ ] Coffee/vending machines
- [ ] Emergency exits and supplies
- [ ] Introduce department staff and key personnel

Position information:

- [ ] Team members and assistants
- [ ] Job assignment and description
- [ ] Training plans
- [ ] Job schedule and hours
- [ ] Family communication
- [ ] Performance expectations and standards

Create the Training Schedule

The structure of the training program allows you to provide a consistent training experience for the director. Over time, if the program is not generating the desired results, you can change your initial training program to improve the experiences. For example, you might learn that you need to provide your director with more time to learn the finance modules or operations.

Divide your training schedule into modules with a clear objective for each module. Offer assessments and opportunities for feedback.

Sample Schedule Director's Training

Day 1

9 a.m. to 9:15 a.m.	Meet and greet
9:15 a.m. to 10 a.m.	Module 1: Introduction to Our Company: Vision, mission, and values of the organization
10 a.m. to 10:30 a.m.	Tour of the facility
10:30 a.m. to 12 p.m.	Module 2: Strategic Planning: » How to run the best program » Introduction to quality control » Owner's operations dashboard » Introduction to director's operations dashboard
12 p.m. to 1 p.m.	Lunch with owner
1 p.m. to 5 p.m.	Orientation: » Learn about the organizational structure » Learn to identify qualities of leaders and managers » Take opportunities for self-reflection » Review director and owner files » Sign paperwork » Review job description » Review staff handbook » Complete leadership assessment

Day 2

8 a.m. to 9:30 a.m.	View health-check, procedure, and videos
9 a.m. to 12 p.m.	Module 3: Customer-Service Dashboard: » Expectations about our service culture » Improvement process » Quality standards » Resources for families » Communicating with families » Parent-teacher conferences » Parent-communication software training » Collections

12 p.m. to 1 p.m.	Lunch break
1 p.m. to 3 p.m.	Review the owner's operations dashboard and strategies
3 p.m. to 5 p.m.	Business-plan fundamentals

Day 3

9 a.m. to 12 p.m.	Operations
	Classroom observations and curriculum checklist
	Complete school-evaluation form
	Complete inspection walkthrough
	Create the director's dashboard
12 p.m. to 1 p.m.	Lunch break
1 p.m. to 6 p.m.	Module 4: Marketing:
	» Enrollment/sales expectations and projections
	» Marketing plan
	» Creating tours for families
	Module 5: Finance:
	» Billing projections
	» Budgets
	» Billing software training

Day 4

9 a.m. to 12 p.m.	Classroom inspections and observations
12 p.m. to 1 p.m.	Lunch break
1 p.m. to 6 p.m.	Module 6: Human-Resources Management:
	» Add SMART goals to job descriptions
	» Define HR and recruitment practices
	» Review new-employee training expectations
	» Explore and discuss mentoring program
	» Discuss conducting interviews, recruiting staff, onboarding and training new employees, coordinating staff meetings, making staff schedules, and authorizing vacation
	» Review staff handbook and staff job descriptions
	» Examine document policies and procedures
	» Discuss pay scales and how to conduct yearly reviews
	» Explain firing procedures and documentation

Day 5

9 a.m. to 12 p.m.	*Create teachers' and assistant teachers' operations dashboards*
12 p.m. to 1 p.m.	*Lunch break*
1 p.m. to 6 p.m.	*Module 7: Operations:*

- » *Review expectations for classroom management and licensing inspections*
- » *Creating classroom schedules*
- » *Ordering furniture and toys*
- » *Review parent handbook*
- » *Making supply orders*
- » *Forms such as fire drills*
- » *Review evacuation routes*
- » *Creating lunch menus*
- » *Making monthly calendars*
- » *Setting up classrooms*
- » *Creating child files*
- » *Review enrollment contracts and enrollment forms*
- » *Documenting building maintenance*
- » *Quality control*
- » *Accreditation*

Step 2: The Director's Onboarding Training

The main goal of the onboarding training is to provide the new director with a checklist of processes, a job description, expectations, and milestones of the business plan. This process starts a couple of months before opening your facility or, if you're hiring a director for an operating school, during the initial onboarding. During this time, the owner works closely with the director to create or review the processes required to run the facility.

The Director's Job Description

Child-care directors are responsible for the day-to-day operations of a child-care center. The responsibilities include ensuring safety standards are met, managing staff, developing curriculum, communicating with families, and meeting licensing requirements. According to Cathleen Yonahara and Mark Schickman in their article for HR Daily Advisor, a job description must contain five critical components:

- Heading information: the job title, pay range, reporting relationship, and hours

- A summary of the objective of the job

- Qualifications: Experience, training, and technical skills

- Special demands: Heavy lifting, for example

- Job duties and responsibilities: tasks listed in order of the time consumed to complete them

Within the job description, the lists of tasks could be assigned to categories such as the following:

- **Sales and marketing:** giving tours, contacting leads, and community outreach

- **Licensing:** compliance and record keeping, such as licensing information, maintaining updated records

- **Finance:** collecting parent payments, managing the budget

- **Human resources:** recruiting staff, onboarding and training new employees, ongoing training, coordinating staff meetings, creating staff schedules, authorizing vacation and leave

- **Quality controls:** conducting classroom observations, assessing children, and monitoring curriculum implementation

- **Customer service:** customer support and communication

- **Operations:** reviewing classroom checklists and ordering supplies

The following is an example:

Child-Care Director Reporting to Owner

Summary of Objective of the Job	To coordinate, budget, and manage the daily successful operation of ABC Child Care following the guidelines of the Department of Family and Protective Services
Qualifications	• Bachelor's degree in education with a concentration in child development or early childhood • Must be able to be certified as a director of a child-care center • Strong organizational and time-management skills • Strong communication, public relations, and interpersonal skills • Strong computer skills • Ability to coordinate center functions • Ability to implement policy and procedures • Comprehensive knowledge and proven success implementing programs for children based on developmentally appropriate practices • Accepts and respects differences in children, families, and coworkers • Ability to manage a budget • Three years of experience as a classroom teacher of young children • Three to five successful years of experience managing child-care facilities • Friendly and approachable demeanor • Able to maintain a professional appearance, attitude, and work ethic at all times
Special Demands	• Able to maintain emotional control under stress • Able to work with frequent interruptions • Able to work occasional prolonged and irregular hours • Able to perform frequent standing, stooping, bending, kneeling, pushing, and pulling movements • Capable of prolonged use of computer and repetitive hand motions • Able to occasionally lift up to 50 pounds

Main Responsibilities and Duties	• Instructional Management: Maintain, at all times, high-quality child-care standards based on developmentally appropriate practices.
	• Personnel Management:
	⋛ Supervise all staff members of the child-care center.
	⋛ Oversee hiring process and orientation for all new staff.
	⋛ Provide accurate and meaningful annual performance evaluations for all child-care staff.
	• Management of Fiscal, Administrative, and Facilities Functions:
	⋛ Develop a budget for the center, and establish controls to ensure that the center adheres to the budget.
	⋛ Ensure that the program is cost effective and funds are managed prudently.
	⋛ Develop and implement policies and procedures for the operation of the child-care center.
	• Operations:
	⋛ Ensure consistent compliance with all minimum standards, including maintenance and preparation for annual fire, health, and other inspections.
	⋛ Coordinate the annual licensing of the child-care center.
	⋛ Oversee the maintenance of files according to requirements.
	• Customer Service:
	⋛ Maintain open, consistent, and effective communication with families, providing family education training, assistance, and support as needed.
	⋛ Use appropriate and effective techniques to encourage community and parent involvement.
	⋛ Collect parent payments.
	⋛ Communicate effectively with staff, students, and their families.
	• Marketing: Provide reliable, accurate, and timely information about the child-care center to interested parties.
	• General:
	⋛ Attain and maintain membership in NAEYC.
	⋛ Assist in other projects as assigned by supervisor.
	⋛ Articulate the center's mission to employees and other stakeholders, and solicit support in realizing the mission.
	⋛ Represent the center in a professional, courteous, and positive manner at all times.
	⋛ Promote a positive, caring climate for learning for staff, students, and families.
	⋛ Deal sensitively and fairly with persons from diverse cultural backgrounds.

BUILD YOUR KNOWLEDGE

Create a list of responsibilities for a director at your school and then organize those responsibilities into categories that meet your needs. Think about tasks such as the following:

» Develop and implement program operating policies and procedures as required.

» Formulate the annual program budget.

» Ensure that the program operates within budgetary parameters established; if circumstances cause budget to exceed or create potential for budget to be exceeded, plan and implement cost-reduction strategies and arrange for increased funding. For example, your actual payroll ratio is higher than your budget estimate (percentage of payroll divided by your total income). As a director, you might need to adjust schedules or increase billing to meet your program goals.

» Plan, develop, schedule, and/or provide in-service training and evaluation of child-care staff.

» Ensure that the center and staff conform to federal, state, and local rules, regulations, and licensing requirements.

» Recruit and hire new employees.

» Supervise new-employee orientation.

» Set up professional goals and yearly evaluations for new employees.

» Conduct regular assessments to evaluate employee performance (teacher inventory).

» Supervise the staff, and ensure that staff members are carrying out their duties.

» Ensure that employees are trained and follow all procedures.

» Organize staff work schedule.

» Establish procedures to ensure that all discipline procedures are in place.

» Conduct staff meetings.

» Authorize staff vacations.

» Coach employees to improve performance.

» Prepare contracts for renewals.

» Terminate employees, if needed.

- » Recruit and schedule children for the child-care center; maintain accurate records on children enrolled in the program, including their development, attendance, immunization, and general health.

- » Conduct program registration, and maintain appropriate files and waiting lists.

- » Ensure that policies and procedures are followed.

- » Monitor and sign children's accident forms.

- » Conduct fire drills and other requirements of state board.

- » Conduct regular safety and building inspections.

- » Comply with state child-care rules and regulations.

- » Prepare yearly paperwork for the state board, and prepare reports for the agencies.

- » Create and maintain updated staff files.

- » Maintain updated children's files.

- » Conduct regular visits to the classrooms.

- » Conduct drills every month as required.

- » Maintain strict confidentiality in regard to children, staff, and families.

- » Maintain CPR and first aid certifications.

- » Maintain bloodborne pathogens and fire-extinguisher class records.

- » Maintain child abuse and neglect records.

- » Host monthly and special events.

- » Deal with parents' complaints in a timely manner.

- » Conduct family surveys.

- » Conduct parent-teacher conferences to address concerns.

- » Coordinate initial parent-teacher meetings.

- » Build relationship with the families.

- » Update social media following the guidelines of the marketing department.

- » Demonstrate cultural sensitivity in communications and work with families and children.

- » Demonstrate an awareness of community resources for additional support of children and families.

- » Send families a monthly newsletter with information about the curriculum, events, and information.

- » Meet with the parents to discuss situations and develop improvement plans.

- » Develop parent education series to support families.
- » Ensure curriculums are being implemented correctly by teachers.
- » Complete KPI forms and procedures.
- » Ensure implementation of successful camps, including field trips.
- » Coordinate administration of measuring tools, including child assessments and internal KPI tools, to ensure quality control.
- » Stay up to date with the accreditation process.
- » Give tours to prospective families.
- » Conduct enrollment analysis.
- » Build waiting lists.
- » Meet the company's financial goals.
- » Collect payments from parents.

Step 3: Delegation Sessions

You have probably been in situations in which you were asked to take responsibility but still had to go back to the expert because you didn't feel empowered to make a decision.

Child-care owners often fall into two main categories: those who fall into the trap of having their directors check with them on every decision, and those who foster an environment where directors can make decisions, ask questions, and complete the job. There are some barriers to delegation, including the belief that you can perform the task yourself or the need to be in control of the ultimate decision.

According to Jesse Sostrin in an article in the *Harvard Business Review*, one of the most difficult transitions for leaders is to shift from doing to leading. Sostrin asserts that, while it may seem difficult, elevating your impact will require you to embrace that you need to lead yet be less involved. Executing work might be holding you back from activating your team and could be a source of frustration with your director, who is eager to take on the responsibility.

If you are ready to effectively delegate the day-to-day operations of your child-care center and design a culture of accountability, the first step is to transfer the strategic goals of your owner's dashboard into your director's operations dashboard. To do this, you will need your operations dashboard (discussed in chapter 2). Your operations dashboard will help you communicate the vision and strategic goals of your business plan in a visual representation. During this training session, communicate the strategic goals of the program, and delegate the tactical goals to the director. The director will assume responsibility for setting action steps and committing to the expectations of the owner.

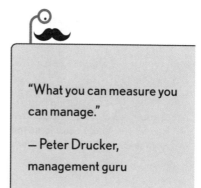

"What you can measure you can manage."

— Peter Drucker, management guru

Start by communicating your vision and strategic goals for each department. Next, ask your director to complete the tactical goal for each strategic goal in the third column of the owner's dashboard using a SMART format. (You can use the sticky-note method from chapter 2 to brainstorm ideas or organize a sequence of events.) Then, add the action steps to each task in order of priority, and add timeline for each action step. The following is an example.

Owner's Dashboard

DEPARTMENT	STRATEGIC GOAL	TACTICAL GOALS	ACTION STEPS	TIMELINE
Sales	Have a waiting list in the first year	Enroll 5 students per month	• Set all leads in automation software for follow-up.	After tours
			• Call leads for follow-up.	Every Wednesday
			• Organize open houses.	Quarterly
Marketing	Become the market leader in the community	• Increase the web page authority by 20 percent in the first year • Generate 20 leads per month with marketing campaign • Have 5 leads referred by families per month	• Send surveys to families.	Quarterly
			• Get 5 family testimonials for the web page.	Monthly
			• Set up campaign budget.	September, then track monthly
			• Track family leads with incentives.	Monthly
Licensing	Have a perfect licensing record	No write-offs or violations		As needed

Finance	Achieve profitability and efficiency; invest in what we value	• Have payroll-to-income percentage lower than 45 percent • Maintain financial ratios	Prepare financial ratios to track	Monthly
Human Resources	Be considered the best place to work	• Turnover rate does not exceed 10 percent • Employee satisfaction is 90 percent • 360-degree reviews are over 90 percent	• Send employee survey • Conduct assessment reviews	Quarterly Monthly
Customer Service and Retention	Have high customer satisfaction and excellent customer-service experiences	• Customer-service metrics, such as CSAT, are over 90 percent • Customer churn is low	• Send out customer survey • Review disenrollment report	Quarterly Monthly
Operations	Have an outstanding reputation in the community	• Test scores of students are at or above 90 percent • Safety procedures are followed • Achieve/maintain accreditation status	Conduct classroom assessments	Weekly

Once your director completes the action steps on the owner's dashboard, she is ready to transfer her tasks to her director's dashboard, her control panel. The director's dashboard is different from the owner's dashboard and includes the KPIs of the job and tasks of the job description. The director's dashboard includes the following:

☑ List of each department

☑ Tactical goals for each department

☑ Action steps written using the SMART (specific, measurable, assignable, relevant, and time-bound) format

- ☑ Person responsible for each action step

- ☑ Timeline for each action step

Transfer the tactical goals from owner's dashboard. Here is an example:

DEPARTMENT	TACTICAL GOAL	ACTION STEPS	PERSON(S) RESPONSIBLE	TIMELINE
Sales	• Enroll 5 students per month	• Set all leads in sales funnel	Assistant director/ receptionist	After every call
	• Call leads for follow-up	• Call prospective families on Wednesdays	Director	Weekly
		• Conduct tours		Monthly
Marketing	• Increase the web page authority by 20 percent in the first year	• Send surveys to families	Director	Quarterly
	• Generate 20 leads per month with marketing campaign	• Get 5 family testimonials for the web page.		Monthly
	• Have 5 leads referred by families per month	• Set up campaign budget.		September, then track monthly
		• Track family leads with incentives		Monthly
		• Review website traffic metrics and Google analytics		Weekly
		• Get one family testimonial		Weekly
		• Conduct SWOT meeting		Monthly

Licensing	No write-offs or violations	• Maintain accurate records on children enrolled in the program, including their development, attendance, immunizations, and general health • Complete licensing report • Compile child assessments and classroom reports • Document center occupancy	Director/Assistant director	Monthly
Finance	• Have payroll-to-income percentage lower than 45 percent • Maintain financial ratios	• Calculate amount billed • Review financial ratios and payroll reports • Calculate payroll as a percentage of revenue • Make enrollment projections	Director/accounts receivable	Weekly
		• Review financial ratios	Director	Monthly
Human Resources	• Turnover rate does not exceed 10 percent • Employee satisfaction is 90 percent • 360-degree reviews are over 90 percent	• Recruit new teachers • Interview 2 candidates	Director	Weekly
		• Calculate turnover rate • Conduct exit interviews • Conduct employee experience survey (recruiting, onboarding, mentoring) • Conduct assessment reviews • Send employee survey • Review employee surveys		Monthly

		• Plan, develop, schedule, and/or provide in-service training and evaluation of staff		Quarterly
Customer Service and Retention	• Customer-service metrics, such as CSAT, are over 90 percent • Customer churn is low	• Start with a baseline customer-service survey to determine areas of opportunity • Conduct parent surveys	Director	Quarterly
		• Review customer-service metrics		Planning session
		• Create a customer journey with staff members		
		• Track disenrollment		
		• Ensure correct implementation of curriculum		Weekly
Operations	• Test scores of students are at or above 90 percent • Safety procedures are followed • Accreditation status has been achieved	**Test Scores:** Track student assessments to identify children with low scores	Director	Weekly
		Safety: Conduct classroom inspections		Monthly
		General: • Conduct staff meetings • Conduct program registration • Review classroom checklists • Order supplies		Weekly
		Accreditation: • Start self-study • Maintain appropriate files and waiting lists		By second quarter Weekly

Next, write a sequence of action steps into a simple format that allows the director to view the frequency in a SMART format. As previously mentioned, Dale Carnegie said, "People help support a world they help create." Duncan Haughey reports in the article "A Brief History of SMART Goals" that business consultant George T. Doran suggested turning goals into SMART goals: *specific, measurable, assignable, relevant,* and *time-bound*, and later, Robert Rubin, a professor at Saint Louis University, further developed the idea, changing *assignable* to *attainable*.

- ▣ **S: Specific**—What, when, where, and how?

- ▣ **M: Measurable**—What data will measure the progress?

- ▣ **A: Assignable**—What are the steps you will take to reach the goal, and who will be responsible for those steps?

- ▣ **R: Relevant**—Does this goal align with your other goals?

- ▣ **T: Time-bound**—What is your time frame for reaching this goal?

For each action step, prioritize tasks and set mini-goals with milestones. The director will monitor and evaluate the action steps on a regular basis. With the SMART format, there is an expectation for every duty, and those expectations are set up by the director herself. By involving the employee in the process, you are transferring responsibility, setting expectations, and reaching a new level in your operations.

Let's create our first SMART goal and deliverables from one of the tasks from the licensing department.

Task: Maintain accurate records on children enrolled in the program, including their development, attendance, immunizations, and general health

Together with your director, break down the task into SMART goals.

- ▣ **Specific:** Create and maintain children's records.

- ▣ **Measurable:**
  - » Create each child's file after the child enrolls in the facility.
  - » Add attendance weekly.
  - » Add development assessment results monthly.
  - » Add immunization records upon enrollment.

□ **Attainable**:

> » Complete files.
> » Input data in the system.
> » Create reminders of immunization expiration dates.

□ **Relevant:** Necessary to maintain licensure

□ **Time-bound:** Update records as needed every week.

Then, establish how to measure the task and the frequency. This is especially important as follow-up meetings set the expectations of the process.

TASK	SMART GOALS	DELIVERABLE TO OWNER
Maintain accurate records on children enrolled in the program to include their development, attendance, immunization, and general health	• Create a file for each child when that child enrolls. • Add attendance, development assessment results, and immunization records. • Input data of expiring immunization records to remind one month before expiration date.	Licensing inspection reports

Step 4: Build Successful Mentoring Relationships

Seasoned directors who have the support of a hands-on owner who views them as partners have a much better chance of aligning the core values and the culture. Directors drive initiatives, but the processes must be owned by every staff member. Mentoring starts at the top of the organization and cascades to every team member.

Help your director create accountability across your organization by designing an onboarding experience that will help build that culture you want to create. Directors are not able to oversee every procedure and process inside a school to ensure consistency in the implementation of high-quality standards. To effectively delegate a responsibility, directors have to first experience empowerment to be able to engage the rest of the team.

HOW TO CONDUCT A POLICY OR PROCEDURE TRAINING

> » Select policy owners and mentors, such as lead teachers.
> » Offer opportunities to practice the skill.
> » Assign mentors to support employees in need of assistance.

» Ask mentors to give feedback to employees.

» Recognize and reward employees in staff meetings to reinforce the importance of the policy or procedure.

Let's take the handwashing procedure as an example. I've heard directors grumble, "We've done this training multiple times. How could they still miss a step?" As a director, you are not able to control whether all teachers at the school are following all the steps. Yet, what you can do is to give the information, train the employee, allow the employee to receive mentorship and to practice, and then establish a control system to oversee the implementation, such as observing the practice from time to time during weekly inspection visits to classrooms. Rewarding best practices is a great way to reinforce expected outcomes during staff meetings or during your visits.

BUILD YOUR KNOWLEDGE

In the onboarding process, the owner will give the director a list of responsibilities, but it is the director's job to fill in the SMART goals for the tasks. Imagine you are creating the chart of responsibilities for your director. Fill it out, then create SMART goals.

	TASKS	SMART GOALS
Sales		
Marketing		
Licensing		
Finance		
Human Resources		
Customer Service and Retention		
Operations		

Step 5: Monitor Progress

Successful child-care centers share the same vision of quality, quantify results, and reward employees based on those results. Owners need to track to evaluate whether their actions are driving the desired outcomes. The keys to quality are consistency in following processes and monitoring results to create accountability.

The best way to monitor results is to use the framework of the dashboard during your weekly meetings with your director. Measures without meetings are useless. This is the opportunity to ask your director specific questions related to your goals and action steps, such as, "What are you doing about this number?" or "What could you do to avoid this situation next time?"

The following is a sample agenda that can be used in your weekly meetings.

Weekly Meeting Agenda

DEPARTMENT	TACTICAL GOAL	ACTUAL RESULTS
Sales		
Marketing		
Licensing		
Finance		
Human Resources		
Customer Service and Retention		
Operations		

Step 6: Analyze Your Data

Once you track and gather your data from all your KPIs, you are ready to examine the information to identify trends and patterns. For example, if your monthly turnover rate is going up and your employee satisfaction scores are going down, that might be an indicator that there is a problem in your human-resources department. If you are not getting enough leads from your marketing initiatives, there is a problem with your marketing campaign or setup. Or if you are getting many leads and tours but they are not converting to sales, this could be a sign that your sales process is not working. Your data will provide you with strategic feedback to adapt and create new action steps to steer the organization in a new direction. Work with your new director to evaluate your KPIs and brainstorm strategies to address any issues you discover.

6

PROFESSIONAL-DEVELOPMENT PLANS FOR OWNERS AND DIRECTORS

_GG_____

God grant me the serenity to accept the people I cannot change, the courage to change the one I can, and the wisdom to know it's me.

—JOHN G. MILLER, *QBQ! THE QUESTION BEHIND THE QUESTION: PRACTICING PERSONAL ACCOUNTABILITY IN WORK AND IN LIFE*

MAIN QUESTIONS

» What are some strategies to mentor a high-performing director?

» What are some important things owners can learn to support directors?

» What are some of the assessment tools you can use to identify areas of opportunity?

TERMS TO KNOW

360-degree assessment: feedback from staff members to help you identify areas of opportunity to grow and improve

Self-awareness: an in-depth knowledge of one's emotions, values, purpose, strengths, drive, abilities, and limitations

---

Leaders recognize areas where they or their organization can improve. On the other hand, people who lack leadership skills blame others for their failures and are unable to identify their areas of improvement. In her *Forbes* article "Are Leaders Born or Made?" Erika Andersen asserts that leadership ability falls along a bell curve. On one end of the curve, she says, are the natural leaders who start out as very good leaders and get even better as they go along. On the other end are the people who will never be very good leaders. The rest fall somewhere in the middle. Andersen says, "Most folks who start out with a modicum of innate leadership capability can actually become very good, even great, leaders."

Case Study: Successful Professional Development

Erika had been running the center for more than a decade. The previous owners were great but did not involve her in the business side of the operation. When I stepped into the building for the first time as the new owner, she encountered a completely different leadership style and mindset. I wanted to include her in the business side.

Erika's biggest challenge as a director was to understand the financial part of the operation, and my responsibility was to mentor her in understanding it. When Erika looked at the financial statements for the first time, she seemed overwhelmed. I translated complex financial concepts and cost ratios, and I mentored her as she developed the skills to understand the statements.

To start with, I gave her an overview of the importance of financial statements. Like photographs, financial statements capture a moment in time. Different statements look at the organization from different perspectives. Together, we reviewed our expenses and revenue expectations, and I encouraged her to ask questions. To build bridges between the business and operations sides of the organization, I explained that owners and investors take on huge risks when opening child-care centers, including the responsibility to guarantee bank loans if the business fails.

Today, Erika creates budgets and projections, and she can give you a lecture from the director's perspective on why programs need to be profitable, with details about budgets and ratios. With hard work, a good attitude, and a professional-development plan, she conquered one of her biggest fears.

According to the article "The Future of Skills: Employment in 2030" by Thomas Vander Ark, research indicates that a diverse background is what is needed for today's upcoming professionals and should include skills that are uniquely human, such as decision making. This perspective is supported in the example of involving Erika in understanding the financial planning of the business, which enabled her to make critical decisions about changes or adjustments on a weekly basis.

When directors understand the relationships, ratios, and business expectations, they are empowered to make decisions to stay within state guidelines and understand the changes they need to make in employee schedules. For example, think about payroll ratio. Payroll represents the biggest expense in a child-care company. The payroll represents a percentage of the weekly income; this percentage is the payroll-to-income ratio. During the COVID-19 pandemic, payroll ratios increased considerably as child-care programs had to hire more teachers because many states required lower teacher-child ratios.

Developing oneself into a leader who inspires others to participate in and expand his vision requires planning, hard work, and dedication. When owners and directors lead by example in developing their learning journeys, employees are inspired to follow.

THE JOURNEY BEGINS WITH SELF-AWARENESS

Self-awareness is an in-depth knowledge of one's emotions, values, purpose, strengths, drive, abilities, and limitations. People who view leadership as a genetic gift might believe that there is no need to improve their skills. On the other hand, most people fall into the category of "leader in the making." If you are aware of your limitations and believe that leadership can be learned with hard work, you can create your improvement plan.

In their book *The Visionary Director: A Handbook for Dreaming, Organizing, and Improvising in Your Center*, authors Margie Carter and Deb Curtis explain that professionals who see themselves as the developers of an organizational culture attract staff and families longing to be involved in this kind of community. Along with that is allowing your staff to grow in a strength-based approach, discovering their learning styles by uncovering their passions. At the core of the sequence of becoming a black-belt director are your core values, your mission, and personal goals.

My career would have turned out completely different had I not taken some risks. I know from experience that, while you might lack the skills and industry knowledge to perform a job, if you have the grit, persistence to endure the challenge, and a strong work ethic, you can design a personal-development plan.

In my early thirties, I applied for a job as the vice president of marketing of a large organization in the telecommunications industry. The problem was that I had no previous experience managing people and no idea what I was doing. To my surprise, the president of the company called me for a second interview, and I almost cried when the offer letter arrived in the mail. I couldn't believe it, as I lacked most of the skills to do the job.

On my first day, I was escorted to an office with a view and met my assistant. I waited for days for someone from human resources to come and give me some idea of what I was supposed to do with the people looking at me though my glass window. No one showed up. I decided to take matters into my own hands and started interviewing the managers in my department: product managers, event managers, salespeople, even a group of engineers from product development. It only took me a couple of days to realize the reason I had been hired: no one in the industry wanted the job! I found this out when one of the promotion managers stepped into my office to tell me that they had a bet on how long I would stay in the company, as the three other people who had accepted the position had resigned within just one year. That was the moment when I was determined to prove them wrong.

There were so many things I had to learn in a short period of time—cell-phone towers, industry KPIs, financial models. My initial approach was to learn the business by conducting one-on-one meetings with team members. Each conversation started with the questions *What are the biggest challenges in your department?* and *How can I add value to your job?* Mayris, the vice president of customer service, gave me a crash course on customer retention. Miguel, the vice president of engineering, drew technological explanations on napkins. Raul, the CEO of the company and a financial guru, explained all the reports in detail. Finally, the regional CEO invested time explaining the vision of the company to me.

Once I had a clear understanding of the strategic goals of the company from a management perspective, I started interviewing staff members one by one to align the strategy to what was happening on a day-to-day basis. I was candid with everyone: *Can you show me what you do so I can understand better how I could help you?* In a short period of time, I had completed needs assessments of their problems and frustrations. I was able to come up with a strategy to help the team based on the strategic goals of the company, my strengths, and the strengths of my team members. For example, Claudia, a product manager, was much better than I was in preparing product descriptions and financial analyses, so I delegated that task completely to her and asked for her to coach me to understand the process. Mike, a tech guru, explained in simple terms the basics of programming and what I needed to know.

Through my conversations with my team members, I discovered that I lacked most of the skills required to perform the job and that some of those things could not be learned in a higher-education institution. Yet, by focusing on my strengths and acknowledging my limitations, I realized that I could get better at specific skills that were not inherent to me. I also became very strategic about the most important skills that I had to learn and could not delegate. Through this process, I was able to design my personal-development plan.

The job that no one wanted proved to be the best investment I have made in my professional career—even more than the formal education I received—and it all just started because I took the risk of accepting a job that no one wanted and I was self-aware of my strengths and limitations.

Owners who lead by example set a culture of self-development that, in turn, builds a culture of mentorship. You are not required to know everything in a school setting, just the areas that pertain to your role in supporting children's learning. Mentoring a high-performing director requires you to build a bridge between both sides— business and operations—of the organization and a partnership in which both parties begin the journey of self-improvement.

The art of becoming a high-performing owner or director lies within you. It starts by understanding your skills, believing in your passion to change the world, reflecting on experiences, and developing a personal-improvement plan to reach one new milestone at a time.

PROFESSIONAL-DEVELOPMENT LEARNING TRACKS FOR OWNERS

To build a bridge with your director, you need to have a working understanding of a variety of topics: rules and regulations, your state's child-care training requirements, your state's child-development standards and expectations, and the accreditation standards.

Rules and regulations: You need to understand your state's teacher-child ratios, regulations regarding background checks, how to complete licensing reports, and your state's safety standards and requirements to operate a child-care center. Your state regulations are closely related to your profitability and set the expectations of what programs need to do to stay in compliance. Have a working understanding of the following:

- The license application

- Background screenings

- Record keeping

- Teacher-child ratios

- Transportation requirements

- Child discipline

- Physical environment requirements of your facility

- Fire safety and emergency preparedness

- Health and safety

Training requirements: Know the requirements for child-care professionals in your state, as hours and annual training requirements vary by state. You can find your state's training requirements on the licensing department website.

Child-development standards and expectations: Have a working knowledge of the rules pertaining to your state's funding requirements and expectations around learning standards and child assessments.

Accreditation standards: Understand the standards by which your state offers accreditation to teachers and directors in early childhood programs. Accreditation is usually required within a specific timeframe from the date of hire. Also have a working knowledge of accreditation standards for programs by groups such as NAEYC.

PROFESSIONAL-DEVELOPMENT LEARNING TRACKS FOR DIRECTORS

A motivated director has the capacity to develop into a high-performing leader. Daniel Goleman, in his 2004 article "What Makes a Leader" in the *Harvard Business Review*, asserts that emotional intelligence is born in the limbic system, which governs "feelings, impulses, and drives." Emotional intelligence is developed best through motivation, extended practice, and feedback. Therefore, leadership training has to engage the limbic system to engage emotions and drive. I believe that if the motivation is there, we can take someone to the next level with a process. For inspiration on how to create a process to help directors become high achievers, I have looked outside our industry to the world of classical-music training.

Practicing a skill many times leads to a certain level of mastery. James Hunt and Joseph Weintraub, coauthors of *The Coaching Manager: Developing Top Talent in Business*, write, "We need to constantly look for opportunities to stretch ourselves in ways that may not always feel comfortable at first. Continual improvement is important to get ahead." My mother would agree. I was a classical pianist and cellist for many years. I started playing the piano when I was just four years old, before I could read or write. My mother oversaw my practice time until she realized I could do it on my own. I spent my childhood and adolescence practicing two hours of piano and two hours of cello every day, including weekends.

My training as a classical musician gave me insights into the work and dedication required to reach a new milestone. Every year, my focus was on gaining new skills through different musical pieces. Over the years, the technical difficulties required more effort, time, and practice. If I didn't put in the work, the outcome would be the same every week. The only way to avoid getting stuck was to put in the work. Even now, I can remember how to play these difficult pieces. My brain trained my muscles, and that information was stored somewhere in my subconscious mind. My process followed a familiar pattern.

Learning any new skill is easier with a few basic tips. Establish the right mindset to start practicing. Allocate a time and space where you can focus and practice regularly. Assess your baseline. Understand your level of skill or knowledge, including your strengths and weaknesses. Identify resources, and follow a program consistently.

1. Break down the challenge into small parts. Practice until you have mastered each section. Breaking a complicated musical piece into small pieces, for

example, allows a musician to master pieces of the content to eventually learn the whole.

2. Observe an expert or mentor doing the task. In learning a piece of music, it helps to listen to a master musician play the piece expertly.

3. Put in the work. Take time to practice. There is no other way than to work hard on a skill.

4. Get feedback from a coach regularly, and seek honest feedback. Musicians meet regularly with their music teachers to seek feedback about the work.

5. After mastering the skills, own it internally. Find your style to make it authentic. For example, once you are able to perform the technical aspects of a musical piece, you are ready to own it and find your style.

6. Showtime! You are ready to share your work with the world.

My music instructor, Slobodan Veljkovic, didn't only teach me music. He taught me how to learn for life and create my personalized learning plan.

HOW TO DESIGN YOUR INDIVIDUALIZED LEARNING JOURNEY

As directors, we are continually designing plans for improvement and designing professional-development plans for our staff members. We often forget that it all starts with us. The most effective way to lead others is to practice skills yourself. Identifying our areas of improvement allows us to create our personalized learning plan.

Successful directors are organized individuals who manage their facility by setting goals. Organizational skills encompass a set of abilities that help a person plan, prioritize, and achieve his goals and include tools and personal organizational management systems.

Develop a Growth Mindset

As James Strock, author of *Serve to Lead*, puts it, leadership is about change. From science, we learn the power of adaptability. Charles Darwin, author of *On the Origin of Species*, held that it is not necessarily the strongest nor the most intelligent who survives but the one who can adapt to change. Make sure you have the right mindset to start the process. Be willing to ask questions, seek feedback, and consider the answers and suggestions. Be willing to listen, learn, and grow.

Use assessment tools to find areas where you could grow. For example, complete a leadership self-assessment, such as the following. Think about these descriptions and areas of skill and how they apply to you. Give yourself a rating of 1 (the lowest level) to 5 (the highest level). Cite some evidence to support the rating you choose for each.

▣ **Passion for the industry:**

» I keep in touch with the families I have served, to track their child's progress.
» Families believe that I have genuine interest and belief in each child's ability.

▣ **Organizational skills:**

» My center records are in compliance.
» I am a multitasker.
» My staff members complete their required training on time.
» I know how to handle my personal finances.
» I am able to prioritize goals.
» I have systems in place to track my key performance indicators.
» I have internal systems in place to update paperwork.
» I have processes in place to onboard new families and staff members.
» I offer my staff members planning time.
» I am task oriented.
» Our facility has well-maintained indoor and outdoor physical environments.
» I don't have a lot of staff scheduling issues.
» I have a pool of substitutes whom I can call to help.
» I have systems in place to address customer issues.

▣ **Communication skills:**

» My policies and procedures are clearly defined and communicated.
» I am comfortable addressing difficult situations with parents and staff.
» My families give me feedback on the program.
» I listen to understand.
» I seek suggestions and input from the whole team.
» I ask questions to gain information.
» I encourage feedback from my team members.
» I communicate respectfully with parents and am sensitive to different families' cultures and values.
» I express information clearly and concisely.

- » My staff members understand the responsibilities, goals, and expectations of their positions.
- » I allow others to talk.
- » I have effective communication skills, including writing proposals and emails.

▣ Personal responsibility:

- » I have a personal mission statement.
- » I know how to learn.
- » I recognize my areas of needed improvement.
- » I am always looking for ways to improve my program.
- » I have successfully completed an accreditation program.
- » I reflect on past mistakes.
- » I see failures as great opportunities for growth.

▣ Interpersonal skills:

- » I respect the values of and differences in others.
- » I create an environment to exchange ideas.

▣ Leadership skills:

- » My staff members want to work for me.
- » I am self-motivated.
- » I don't let emotions get the best of me.
- » I see change as an opportunity to grow.
- » I adapt to change easily.
- » I enjoy helping others learn.
- » I request feedback to improve performance.
- » I am not emotional.
- » I separate emotions from facts.
- » I offer my staff members mentoring and support.
- » I offer my staff members professional-development opportunities.
- » My staff is able to give feedback on areas of needed improvement in the school.
- » My staff members are involved in setting program goals and measuring progress.
- » I have a professional-development plan and internal promotion plans in place to develop my staff members.
- » I am competent in identifying community resources.
- » I remain objective when conducting improvement sessions.
- » I am able to motivate my staff members to set a high standard.
- » I recognize my strengths, weaknesses, drives, and values.
- » I am able to control and redirect disruptive impulses.

- » I am able to understand people's emotions.
- » I am able to build rapport with others to move them in desired directions.

▣ Process skills:

- » I use time-management techniques.
- » I use a planning process.
- » I know how to delegate effectively.
- » I create job descriptions and expectations.
- » I use organization tools to improve performance.
- » I have effective hiring and training processes in place.
- » I have effective staff scheduling systems in place.
- » I use technology to facilitate process skills.
- » I have a recruiting process to hire competent staff members.
- » I have a process for conducting classroom observations every week.
- » I have a system to oversee curriculum implementation.

▣ Accountability:

- » I have systems in place to hold my team accountable for performance.
- » I have KPIs to track performance.
- » I conduct yearly reviews with employees.
- » I set up goals for each staff member and for the school.
- » I am able to maintain my accountability, confidence, and self-awareness.
- » I model responsible and respectful personal behavior.

▣ Content knowledge:

- » I demonstrate knowledge of pedagogy.
- » I demonstrate knowledge of technology.
- » I know how to identify sources of information.
- » I understand instructional strategies.
- » I have knowledge of classroom management.
- » I demonstrate knowledge of expected outcomes, such as school-readiness scores, with funding sources.
- » I am familiar with organizations within our industry.
- » I am competent in finding community resources.
- » I demonstrate evidence of quality standards.
- » I am up-to-date on current research.
- » I understand the legal structure of the organization.
- » I understand the financial aspects of the operation.
- » I understand social services and health care.

- » I understand our financial statements.
- » I understand our performance indicators.

You can also gain valuable input by conducting a 360-degree assessment. For example, you could reword the statements in the leadership self-assessment, such as, "Marnie demonstrates understanding of current research." Ask your staff members to help you identify areas of opportunities for growth and improvement.

Staff surveys are also a great source of information. Your culture begins with your employees' well-being. You may have heard the saying, "When momma's happy, everyone is happy." Mrs. Gloria, one of our infant teachers, explains it in simpler terms: "Happy teachers, happy children, happy momma." For example, ask your staff questions, such as the following:

- ▣ Are you happy?
- ▣ Are you grateful?
- ▣ Are your leaders reliable?
- ▣ Do you think we hold high standards?
- ▣ Do we provide positive feedback?
- ▣ Do you trust other teachers?
- ▣ Do we provide you with the resources to do your job?
- ▣ Do you feel overwhelmed with classroom management?
- ▣ Do you believe your director is a strong leader?
- ▣ Are you having fun at work?
- ▣ Do you think you have knowledge of child development?
- ▣ Do you show an understanding of developmental milestones and standards?
- ▣ Do you leave your personal problems at the door?
- ▣ Do you smile often?
- ▣ What is the best part of your job?
- ▣ Do you go the extra mile without being asked?
- ▣ Do you believe your team members would do anything for you?
- ▣ Do you warmly greet anyone with whom you come into contact?

- ⊡ Do you care about what you're doing?

- ⊡ Do you feel you are making a difference?

- ⊡ Do we share your enthusiasm?

- ⊡ Do you experience negative emotions sometimes?

- ⊡ Do you have a positive attitude?

- ⊡ Are you somebody who is an asset to the program?

- ⊡ Are you somebody you would like to work with?

- ⊡ Do you believe your colleagues work together to create experiences for the children?

Conduct parent surveys every quarter via email or online. Include accreditation, marketing, and customer-service questions. The survey responses will help you track your performance. You can also call your customers and ask them for feedback over the phone or conduct face-to-face informal surveys during pick-up times. You might discover that some of your areas of weakness are the same areas of improvement for your center. For example, a director who struggles to organize paperwork might have low scores in organizational skills. A director who scores low in communication skills will likely be leading a team that lacks consistency.

Identify Critical Areas of Opportunity

Read and think about the responses and information you gain from the assessment tools.

1. Transfer the lowest results of your self-assessments into your training tracking system.

2. Establish your priorities by the rating scores you receive.

3. Use the goal to establish a vision for the area of improvement.

4. Brainstorm possible solutions, resources, and set specific steps to achieve goals.

5. Implement your plan, and set a timeframe for completion. If the plan will take a long time to complete, set checkpoints to evaluate your progress. To keep accountability in the process, work with the child-care owner or a mentor to help you stay on track.

6. Finally, take time to reflect on your experiences, take notes, write in a journal, or take pictures to document your learning journey.

Use the results to identify your areas of opportunity. For example, let's say that you have gathered information and have identified some opportunities for growth in the following areas:

- ▣ Organizational skills

- ▣ Communication skills

- ▣ Personal responsibility

- ▣ Leadership skills

- ▣ Process skills

- ▣ Content knowledge

AREA OF GROWTH OPPORTUNITY	AREA OF IMPROVEMENT	RATING	EVIDENCE	GOAL	NEXT STEPS	TIMELINE
Organizational skills	I offer my staff members planning time.	3	Staff surveys reflect that staff need more planning time.	Improve that score	Take a time-management class	1st quarter
Communication skills	I am comfortable addressing difficult situations with parents and staff.	1	I avoid meeting with parents when I know there's a difficult situation.	Control my emotions during difficult conversations	Take the Becky Bailey class	2nd quarter
Personal responsibility	I have successfully completed an accreditation program.	5	I have not started the self-study.	Obtain accreditation	• Take the accreditation class • Block 2 hours a day to complete tasks related to accreditation	4th quarter
Leadership skills	I see change as an opportunity to grow.	3	I do not feel comfortable with the pace of change.	Use tools to adapt to change	Read books on growth mindset	1st quarter
Process skills	• I have a recruiting process to hire competent staff members. • I use technology to facilitate process skills.	3	• Our turnover rate is higher than it should be. • I am not comfortable using our software.	Have a recruiting process to hire competent staff members Learn how to use our software effectively	Reduce our turnover rate	2nd quarter
Accountability	I have KPIs to track performance.	4	Understand important metrics in the industry	Benchmark reports for childcare.		
Content Knowledge	I demonstrate knowledge of expected outcomes, such as school-readiness scores, with funding sources.	2	Children are scoring low in literacy.	Understand current research on early literacy	• Attend sessions on literacy at the NAEYC conference in November • Take online training on literacy • Read resource books on how children develop literacy skills	

PERSONAL PROFESSIONAL DEVELOPMENT IN ACTION

One of my biggest challenges was to learn the skill of self-regulation. My family genetics didn't help. Coming from an Italian family, I grew up surrounded by a community who provided role models for how to respond to a trigger. We called it the *cinque minuti di Italiani* (five Italian minutes), which is the permission to lose your temper in an emotional outburst for the first five minutes after an incident. I grew up seeing displays of emotions from my grandfather, my father, my aunt, and many others in our family. As a general policy, we also learned to disregard any comment or reaction to the person who lost his temper. At the end of the accepted five-minute timeframe, the person would regain self-composure and everyone would have already forgotten what triggered the incident. But I grew up to realize that not all people are Italians, and most don't have the same forgiveness policy.

Denial is the biggest hurdle to overcome. I could have blamed my family genetics, but I decided to accept my area of improvement and reframe my story with a new vision. I realized that I couldn't do it by myself, so I recruited mentors and coaches to help me model this essential leadership skill.

Over the years, I have had many opportunities to practice that skill to become much better at dealing with other people's lack of self-control. I am happy to report that I am getting better at my own self-control, in spite of a few relapses. Looking back, I realize that I have been training on the skill for a long time. In my previous career, I mastered it by helping angry customers. Then, I had the opportunity to practice with colleagues, a boss, and a partner who lacked any emotional control or professionalism.

Marnie's Learning Plan

Identify a critical area of opportunity.	Self-regulation
Visualize a goal.	I am able to self-regulate my emotions to communicate clearly.
Learn.	Read Becky Bailey's *Conscious Discipline* program and other self-regulation books.
Find a coach.	I am going to ask Abel for his mentorship.
Practice.	Engage with my mentor in role-playing challenging conversations.
Document.	I am going to keep a diary of my responses.
Reflect.	I will monitor my own behavior, the influences on my behavior, and the consequences of my behavior.

BUILD YOUR KNOWLEDGE

Now it is your turn to create your individualized learning plan.

1. Do a self-assessment, using the questions listed on pages 107-110.

2. Identify three areas of opportunity.

3. Visualize your solutions and goals.

4. Plan how you will learn in each area.

5. Set a timeframe for each goal.

6. Choose a coach or mentor to hold you accountable.

7. Practice your skills.

8. Document the learning process.

9. Reflect.

7

DESIGNING YOUR EMPLOYEES' JOURNEY EXPERIENCE

_____ 66 _____

As you begin changing your thinking, start immediately to change your behavior. Begin to act the part of the person you would like to become. Take action on your behavior. Too many people want to feel, then take action. This never works.

— JOHN MAXWELL, AUTHOR, SPEAKER, AND PASTOR

"If you don't like something, change it. If you can't change it, change your attitude."

— MAYA ANGELOU, AUTHOR AND CIVIL RIGHTS ACTIVIST

MAIN QUESTIONS

» Why is the employee experience important?

» How do you attract the best candidates to your company?

» What is your core positioning statement?

» What are the new trends in the workforce?

» What is recruitment sourcing?

TERMS TO KNOW

Employer branding: the way you engage with prospects through different channels, job boards, and career sites, and give them "reasons to tune in" experiences

Employee engagement: an employee's involvement with, commitment to, and satisfaction with work

Employee survey: a questionnaire to obtain opinions and reviews and to evaluate employee mood and morale, degree of engagement, and to monitor employee achievements

Job description: a formal account of an employee's responsibilities

Leader: the person who leads or commands a group or organization

Manager: a person responsible for controlling or administering all or part of a company or similar organization

New-employee onboarding: the process of integrating a new employee with a company and its culture, as well as giving a new hire the tools and information needed to become a productive member of the team

Policy: a course or principle of action adopted or proposed by a government, party, business, or individual

Procedures: established or official ways of doing something

Search engine optimization (SEO): a method of maximizing the number of visitors to a particular website by ensuring that the site appears high on the list of results returned by a search engine

Self-awareness: a conscious knowledge of one's own character, feelings, motives, and desires

Staff handbook: a book given to employees by an employer; can be used to bring together employment- and job-related information that employees need to know

---

Case Study: The Worst-Ever Staff Party

One year, our management team had had a particularly challenging time as we shifted our attention from running established schools to opening new centers. Our staff did not have the experience in leadership to include every staff member in the process.

Our staff holiday party is typically considered one of the most important events of the year. But the moment we entered the party venue, we knew it was going to be a disaster. Before the event, I had overheard some employees complaining about the selection of the venue—a children's birthday-party site—but we didn't intervene, as we had delegated the party planning task to administrators. Seven out of forty employees showed up, including the three administrators who had organized the party!

We waited for hours for more staff members to arrive. No one did. Our management team started texting other team members to join us at an after-party at a local restaurant. Our staff members responded positively, and we did end up having a great time and creating fun memories.

I learned a lesson from this experience: the employee experience begins by understanding what your employees need, value, and want.

UNDERSTANDING THE EMPLOYEE EXPERIENCE

The employee experience covers every aspect of an employee's interactions with your company, beginning before the person is officially hired and continuing throughout the individual's employment. Let's start by understanding why it is important for customer-centered organizations such as child-care centers to use the employee experience as the foundation for their customer-service strategy. Psychology professor Thomas Gilovich studies the effects of experiences on human decisions. Over the last several decades, he has focused on experiments from real-world evidence to conclude that happiness is derived from our experiences, not things. This includes the experiences in our jobs and the level of employee engagement.

To design your employee experience, you have to lay a solid foundation and align your organization's mission to the rest of the employee journey. Today's employees have a voice through social-media networks and career sites and are ready to share the real culture of organizations with others. Aligning your mission with your brand requires planning, team building, motivation, monitoring, and performance tracking.

There are several steps involved in designing the employee experience for child-care organizations. From the moment a prospect comes across your brand to recruiting to termination, every step of the process is part of your employee experience. Furthermore, you have to understand your ideal candidate's expectations and commit to creating a great place to meet those expectations.

In his article "The Incalculable Value of Finding a Job You Love," Cornell professor Robert Frank highlights one of the most important conditions of job satisfaction: how employees feel about the employer's mission. You cannot fake authenticity—who you are and how you feel. I've had the opportunity to lead great teams committed to our company's mission and have surrounded myself with professionals who are part of my network and circle of friends. I've also experienced the effects of toxic company culture and have refused to be part of a dysfunctional team, out of respect for the employees, children, and families. In both cases, I was in control of the outcome.

For dysfunctional organizations and teams, it is just a matter of time until things unfold to reflect the real values of a company. As we discuss in chapter 3, the culture, mission, and vision of a company always go back to management. Child-care centers that are solely profit driven most likely have owners and directors who place profits over people. Compassionate child-care centers, on the other hand, have owners who deeply care about their staff and families. The good news is that you can have both profit and compassion if you prioritize your people and have a solid business plan. I know from experience that allowing your mission to come to life and designing the employee experience so you attract the right employees requires that you be authentic.

The owner must make it her personal mission to commit to a customer service–centered approach to human resources. Designing the employee experience begins with how closely the owner and the management team follow the guiding principles of your core positioning statement and grows with your commitment to protecting the culture of a school where everyone is inspired to come to work, starting with you.

Understand what your employees value. You might be surprised by what your employees truly want. Companies that invest in understanding the values of employees focus on finding ways to support employees' personal goals, develop leadership styles, and reward efforts. Hiring and developing staff has evolved from simply hiring a person to perform a job to focusing on people, what they value, and how they feel about the organization. To do this, you must design the employee experience through the lens of understanding the employees, what they value, and what they need. What you have to offer as an employer is something employees value beyond financial compensation. It could be recognition, the opportunity to shape the next generation, or just a great staff holiday party.

Write Your Core Positioning Statement

Start with your core positioning statement. According to a blog post by Meredith Hart on HubSpot.com, core positioning statements should be brief, unique, and memorable; remain true to business values; and include a promise of what the brand delivers. Try creating one for your company by thinking about the following questions:

- ▣ Who is the target market?

- ▣ What is the target market looking for/what is the need?

- ▣ What do you offer?

- ▣ What is the main benefit you offer to your target market?

- ▣ Why should they believe you offer that benefit?

Then, fill in the blanks:

> For_____ (your target market) who _____ (target need), _____(your brand) provides a _____(main benefits that differ from competitors') because _____ (reason why target market should believe your differentiation statement).

Here is the core positioning statement for our company:

> For working parents in our community who are looking for educational preschool programs that prepare children for school, Young Innovators Academy provides educational learning programs taught by caring certified teachers committed to giving each child the skills to succeed in school and life.

Check Employee Alignment with the Positioning Statement

Once you have defined your core positioning statement, the next step is to align every employee to your mission, starting with your current employees. If you are disappointed about the quality of prospects at your center or the level of disengagement among your staff, you have some groundwork to do before you can lay the foundation of your recruitment strategy.

According to author Jacob Morgan, there are three categories of employees:

- **Actively disengaged:** unhappy employees

- **Not engaged:** sleepwalking through the day

- **Engaged:** working with a passion that feels connected to the organization

To find out the level of engagement of your employees, conduct an employee survey or interview each employee. During the process, you might find that some teachers, such as the ones who are sleepwalking in the hallways or complaining in the staff room, are not engaged and do not fit the culture you want to create. There is a reason you should start categorizing your core team. Engaged employees are likely to refer others to the organization and to share your content on social channels or by word of mouth. Disengaged employees do not believe your core positioning statement is real and are the ones hurting your culture and brand.

The goal is to identify your best employees, turn disengaged employees into passionate team members, or plan termination for those who do not fit your culture. It takes only one negative person or one disengaged employee to alter the course of the journey.

DESIGNING THE EMPLOYEE EXPERIENCE

When you understand what your employees need, want, and expect, you can begin to develop an employee experience to support your team and meet their needs and expectations. I believe there are nine steps to designing the employee experience you want.

1. Attract talent.

2. Recruit.

3. Interview.

4. Plan pre-onboarding.

5. Onboard your new hire.

6. Conduct your tactical plan meeting.

7. Develop and assess your team.

8. Reward dedication and achievement.

9. Offer a positive exit when needed.

Step 1: Attract Talent

The employee experience begins before prospects apply to a job and includes every single touch point during the process. Just like consumers, candidates conduct an online search for job openings. You attract the right candidates with your reputation, commitment to your mission, and a proven track record as a great place to work.

Today, potential employees have changed the way they recruit. There are two very important groups of people who can attract the right pool of prospects: current employees and customers. According to Glassdoor's article "Building an Employer Brand from Scratch," prospects report that they seek company reviews and ratings before deciding to apply for a job, and 69 percent of active job seekers are likely to apply for a job if the employer manages its employer brand, instead of letting the public define the brand. Strong brands can convert prospects into employees.

Employees are empowered to choose companies. Most likely, they will select a company that has a clear understanding of who they are attracting; engages potential employees through their channels; and provides a constant communication strategy on social media, blogs, or newsletters.

One considerable advantage to this shift to online connections is that it enables employers to reduce advertising and career costs through content marketing and social media to reach active job seekers.

Recruiting engaged and passionate educators requires a powerful message of impact. In the new era of the gig economy, talented professionals are choosing to join startups, change careers, pursue their passion or alternative options rather than join established businesses solely for monetary compensation. Everyone wants to play for a winning team.

Purpose-driven generations and professionals are motivated by a mission. By understanding what motivates your ideal candidate, you can craft a powerful message to connect with employees who will propel your mission.

You will start attracting a larger number of qualified candidates as you craft employer-brand messages to share your culture through career pages, newsletters, and job boards. Use stories to share your culture and engage candidates. For example, tell stories about topics such as the following:

- History of the school: perhaps share an inspiring story of the founder who wanted to make a difference

- Teachers delivering exceptional service

- The mission of the school

- Success stories from the classroom

Step 2: Recruit

New trends in the workforce—particularly in a post-pandemic world—require organizations to adopt human-centered principles to stay competitive:

- Changing demographics

- Changing technology

- New behaviors in the marketplace

- Globalization

Even though times have changed, many child-care centers continue to recruit the same way they have for decades: posting job openings, interviewing potential candidates, and hiring. In the past, job seekers used to rely on classified ads and word of mouth. Today, sourcing candidates involves access to search engines, social media, and recruiting websites.

Changing Demographics

Many directors say that managing people is one of the most challenging aspects of their job. The reality is that it is hard to identify, connect, and motivate a new generation of workers and lead a multigenerational workforce.

For years, we have been trying to figure out how to hire and motivate millennials. This generation born between 1982 and 2000 is known, rightly or wrongly, as the trophy kids of helicopter parents and as people who have a reputation for being entitled, self-centered, and immature. Yet, under the right leadership, tech-savvy millennials can become the biggest allies of your company to help you adapt to the new generation of parents.

Changing Technology

The internet has opened up many options for recruiting, such as mobile devices, videoconferencing, and social networks. And job seekers are changing the rules of engagement. From the moment a candidate clicks a post through the application process to the hiring interview, you start creating your employee experience. Today, you have to attract the attention of job seekers with a good marketing message. You must engage applicants through texting or instant messaging and possess the technical skills to optimize your company on search engines.

New Behaviors in the Marketplace

A big shift is underway and will require organizations to change and adapt constantly. During the pandemic, thousands of child-care workers lost their jobs due to the economic hardships imposed on businesses. Even successful child-care centers had to let go of valuable staff members to survive.

As we transition to leading child-care organizations of the future, we will need to become students of behavioral trends. According to Ira S. Wolfe in his book *Recruiting in the Age of Googlization*, the workplace is changing in several ways:

- **Change is constant.** The presumption that employers offer stable jobs is a myth. Professional relationships will be short term, transactional, and unpredictable.

- **Anything can become obsolete at any time.** Every aspect of our business can be impacted without notice by the pace of technological advances.

- **Job security is history.** Organizations will have to respond to market shifts.

- **The free-agent mindset rules.** Free agency is no longer a stigma but a career strategy.

- **Managing people will get harder.**

Globalization

New trends in remote work will introduce new ways of delivering content. As a result of technological advancements in communication, globalization will restructure the way we work, provide employment flexibility, and enable outsourcing of jobs to remote employees who can be hired at the lowest possible cost.

Recruitment Audit

So, how do you learn to recruit in this new environment? Conduct a recruitment audit. A recruitment audit allows owners to improve internal processes. Think about the ways you are currently trying to reach well-qualified job candidates. There are many recruiting channels—some more effective than others. Let's audit your recruitment strategy to find out what is working and what is not.

- ☑ Take a look at the following list. Which resources are you using to find and recruit candidates?
    - » Social media: Facebook, LinkedIn, Instagram, Twitter, YouTube, Snapchat
    - » Industry-specific organizations: NAEYC, AEYCs, National Head Start, Childhood Education International, Child Care Aware of America, DEC, Military Child Education Coalition, National Association for Family Child Care, National Black Child Development Institute, Zero to Three
    - » Professional recruiting company
    - » Referral bonuses to employees
    - » Networking events
    - » Free resources such as university job boards or community boards
    - » Signs outside the building
    - » Local organizations and licensing authorities
    - » Job boards: CareerBuilder, Glassdoor, Indeed, Craigslist, SimplyHired, Monster, ZipRecruiter, Google for Jobs

- ☑ Next, ask yourself the following questions.
    - » How much are you investing every month?
    - » How many candidates are referrals?
    - » Do you find good leads in networking events in your community?
    - » Of the social-media platforms you use to promote your job openings, how many applications do you get per platform? How many recruits do you get?
    - » Are you using an applicant-tracking system to screen applicants?
    - » What happens after someone applies?
    - » Do people apply for the job in person?
    - » Do you contact unqualified candidates?

Once you receive applications through sourcing, you will contact qualified candidates for an interview and disregard unqualified candidates. In the employee experience, even those unqualified candidates are part of the employee journey. Therefore, as a best practice, make it a habit to contact unqualified candidates to thank them for applying to your company.

Step 3: Interview

One common challenge directors have is the "interview no-show" scenario. Many directors are getting more creative in conducting interviews via platforms such as Zoom. Still, there will be some prospects who do not show up. Therefore, to maximize your time, you might consider conducting a quick phone interview as a step before the main interview or coming up with an alternative solution.

As an industry, we have developed great technical questions to vet prospects. What we often fail to include, however, are questions to determine whether the candidate is a good cultural fit. Author Mark Murphy, in his book *Hiring for Attitude*, describes how his company tracked twenty thousand new hires over three years. Within their first eighteen months, 46 percent of them failed (got fired, received poor performance reviews, or were written up). The study showed five categories of characteristics in which failed new hires fell short:

- **Coachability:** the ability to accept and implement feedback from others

- **Emotional intelligence:** the ability to understand and manage one's own emotions and recognize those of others

- **Motivation:** the drive to achieve one's potential

- **Temperament:** an attitude and personality suited for the job

- **Technical competence:** functional or technical skills

Technical competence only accounted for 11 percent of fails. The study showed that someone was a bad hire, in most cases, because the person was not coachable or did not fit the culture of the organization.

Ask any director to list the characteristics of disengaged employees, and she will likely include the following: negative attitude, gossiping, sense of entitlement, blaming others, procrastination, and a love of drama. Ask her to describe an engaged, high-performing employee, and she will likely list a self-directed learner, a team player, and someone with emotional intelligence and an optimistic attitude.

Categorize the characteristics of your high performers and your low performers. Then, with your director, brainstorm scenarios that could help you identify the category a prospect falls into. For example, you could ask, "Can you tell me about a time you were asked to step into another classroom to fill in for a teacher?" A high performer might answer that he has no problem stepping into any task. A low performer might tell you that he prefers to work in a specific group, or he is not willing to perform extra chores.

BUILD YOUR KNOWLEDGE

Brainstorm possible answers to the following questions for both categories of employees: high performer and low performer.

» Can you tell me about a time when you received a write-up at your job?

» Can you tell me about a time when you heard a story about another coworker that affected the school? What did you do?

» Can you tell me what would you do if you saw an employee not following a proper procedure, such as diaper changing?

» Can you tell me what you would do if your supervisor asked you to sign a write-up for not following a process?

Once you brainstorm all scenarios that could help you categorize candidates, identify possible answers that could indicate a poor fit with your organization. Include this cultural-fit assessment in the prospect's file for future reference. Record the answers to the questions to identify which column the candidate falls into.

Step 4: Plan Pre-onboarding

Consider the following as you plan to get your new hire ready for the first day.

Prepare a warm welcome. Consider sending a video, text, or voice mail to let her know how happy you are to have her on your team. Provide information on parking and an orientation checklist. Have the staff handbook, email, software, and classroom space ready.

Plan the training schedule and onboarding checklist. Include time for reviewing the staff handbook, touring the facility, meeting the team, and discussing the curriculum.

Step 5: Onboard Your New Hire

It takes a long time for a new employee to learn a program and its procedures and curriculum. Designing the onboarding experience for a new employee requires directors to involve all staff members in the process. According to SHRM, new-employee onboarding is the process of integrating a new employee with a company and its culture, as well as getting a new hire the tools and information needed to become a productive member of the team. Staffing experts say that onboarding new hires at an organization should be a strategic process and that it should last at least one year. A new recruit should experience different opportunities to engage with new content while receiving coaching with a peer or a mentor. How employers handle the first few days and months of a new employee's experience is crucial to ensuring high retention.

Your onboarding checklist should include a training timeline, any required paperwork, a job description, a facility tour, a staff handbook, and any other important documents or information.

Sample Orientation and Training Timeline

The following is a sample schedule and training timeline for the new hire. The new employee will need to sign a copy of the schedule at the end of the training days for your records.

Day 1

8:30 a.m. to 9 a.m.	Video tour and introductions
9 a.m. to 12 p.m	Staff handbook review
12 p.m. to 1 p.m	Lunch
1 p.m. to 3 p.m.	Policies and procedures
3 p.m. to 5 p.m.	Curriculum training, classroom management

Day 2

8 a.m. to 8:30 a.m.	Director's tour and welcome
8:30 a.m. to 9 a.m.	Paperwork
9 a.m. to 12 p.m.	Circle time and classroom observation
12 p.m. to 1 p.m	Lunch
1 p.m. to 1:30 p.m.	Orientation checklist
1:30 p.m. to 2 p.m.	Job description and goal-setting orientation
2 p.m. to 5 p.m.	Lead-teacher training

I have received two-day orientation training.

Employee's Signature: _____

Employee's Date of Hire: _____ *Date of Orientation:* _____

Trainer's Signature: _____

After the training and orientation, send a survey to the new recruit. Ask her to rate the training on a scale of 1 to 10 (1 being the lowest and 10 being the highest):

- ☑ How informative was your training?

- ☑ How knowledgeable was your trainer?

- ☑ How friendly was your trainer?

- ☑ How professional was your trainer?

- ☑ How well did the trainer tailor the information to the age group you will be teaching?

Checklist for New Employees

Task	Reviewed
Introduce staff members, including auxiliary members.	
Visit all rooms in the school.	
Show locations of fire-escape routes, fire-drill procedures, the locations and operation of fire extinguishers, the location of emergency phone numbers, and review the procedure for emergencies.	
Tour the playground.	
Visit the laundry area and discuss procedures.	
Show all exit routes.	
Review deep-cleaning procedures.	
Show storage areas, including those for resource files and books.	
Review entry procedures.	
Review safety procedures.	

Show the staff room(s).	
Review the job description.	
Review the staff handbook.	

» *The trainer took the time to introduce me to all the classroom areas.*

» *I have been introduced to the school family and have visited all the rooms in the school.*

Employee's Signature: _____

Employee's Date of Hire: _____ Date of Orientation: _____

Trainer's Signature: _____

After the tour, send a survey to the new recruit. Ask her to rate the tour on a scale of 1 to 10 (1 being the lowest and 10 being the highest):

☑ Were you welcomed by your tour guide right away and didn't have to wait around for someone to meet with you? _____

☑ Did you feel welcome by other staff members? _____

☑ Was your tour guide knowledgeable? _____

Staff Handbook Review for New Staff Members

Before starting in the classroom, give a copy of your staff handbook to the new staff member to use as a reference throughout the orientation. Before starting their employment, new employees must complete the following training.

Staff Handbook Checklist

Task	Reviewed
Job responsibilities and information regarding to whom they report	
Policies and procedures listed in the standards that relate to the staff member's responsibilities	
Daily health-screenings procedures	
Playground and outdoor learning safety procedures and plan	

Planning time	
Child and family confidentiality policies and procedures	
Uniform and health code	
Transportation safety policies	
Personal appearance policy	
Food policy	
Policies for telephones, cell phones, and computers	
Daily schedule review	
Emergency and natural disasters training	
Procedures for action in case of ill or injured children and medical emergencies	
Policy for communicating an emergency situation to families	
Policies for infants	
Nap time policy and procedures	
Classroom procedures	
Teacher supply list	
Personal possessions policy	
Policies for the arrival and departure of children	
Inclement weather policy	
Medication and medical procedures policy	
Policy regarding application of sunscreen, diaper ointment or cream, insect repellent	
Infection-prevention procedures	
Handwashing procedure	
Record keeping	
Discipline policies, including acceptable and unacceptable discipline measures	

Communication with families	
Behavioral management	
Termination policies	
Expectations for adult interactions	
Procedures for supervising a child who may arrive after any scheduled classes or activities, including field trips	
Procedures for storing and giving children's medications	
Accident policy	
Hands-on training: » Universal precautions procedures » Activity adaptations » Medication administration » Disabilities precautions and health issues » Appropriate intervention strategies	
Opportunity to observe in classroom of teacher who is a good role model	
Classroom organization expectations, including labeling of all toys	

I have received training in my job responsibilities, and I have been provided a copy of the staff handbook, including all policies and procedures.

Employee's Signature: _____

Employee's Date of Hire: _____ Date of Orientation: _____

Trainer's Signature: _____

Review the job description with the new employee to be sure that she understands her responsibilities. The following is a sample traditional job description.

We are looking for a patient, attentive Day-Care Worker to care for children. The Day-Care Worker will assist parents and the company by preparing meals for children; maintaining children's hygiene; monitoring them for health, behavioral, and emotional concerns; providing them with age-appropriate instruction; and working with families to ensure that children are learning and socializing in a positive way. They may also assist with sterilizing toys and play areas and other duties to ensure that the children are in a safe, engaging, and clean environment.

To be successful as a Day-Care Worker, you should be thorough and caring with an eye for detail. You should be prepared to meet the physical demands of the position and understand the childhood-development process.

Day-Care Worker Responsibilities:

» *Providing care for children, such as setting schedules and routines, grooming, feeding, changing diapers, and cleaning rooms and toys*

» *Developing and encouraging age-appropriate learning and socialization to ensure children learn basic skills and concepts, such as communication, manners, sharing, and so on*

» *Maintaining a safe workplace by monitoring children for health, behavioral, and emotional issues and reporting concerns to staff and families*

» *Helping children discover new interests by introducing them to art, music, sports, and other potential hobbies*

» *Ensuring children are learning positive behaviors and providing guidance or approved discipline, as needed*

» *Preparing children to enter the next level of care or for entry into school*

» *Assist director in mentoring new teachers*

» *Keeping records relating to child care, such as incident reports*

» *Working with families to help children progress toward educational and behavioral goals*

Day-Care Worker Requirements:

» *High school diploma or equivalent*

» *More education and experience may be required or preferred*

» *A valid driver's license*

» *Decisiveness, patience, and stamina to chase after, lift, or carry children*

» *Record of immunizations and ability to pass a background check*

» *Exceptional communication, teaching, and interpersonal skills*

» *Strong understanding of stages of childhood development*

» *Attentiveness to the needs and safety of children*

Some companies or states may have a minimum age requirement.

Additional licenses, certifications, or training may be beneficial or required.

Step 6: Conduct Your Tactical Plan Meeting

An owner needs buy-in from the director in the same way a director requires buy-in from the rest of the team. Work with your team to create a SMART job description and operations dashboards for your teachers. Use your director's dashboard and the caregiver job description.

Teacher's Operations Dashboard

	TASK	GOAL	SMART GOALS	MEASURE
Operations	• Provide care for children, such as grooming, feeding, changing diapers, and cleaning rooms and toys • Provide care for children, such as setting schedules and routines	Consistently follow your classroom schedule.	• Diaper changes are recorded in an app immediately. • Teachers follow the classroom schedule and plan their lesson plans every Friday.	Track app Track documentation of learning experiences
Health and Safety	Monitor children for health, behavioral, and emotional issues and report concerns to staff and families	Maintain a safe workplace.	Implement morning daily health checks.	Daily Track forms
Curriculum	Develop and encourage age-appropriate learning and socialization to ensure children learn basic skills and concepts.	Plan curriculum ahead of time.	Teachers conduct pre- and post-assessments on a monthly basis.	Review children's assessments with director on a monthly basis.
Licensing	Keep records relating to child care.	Use binder for each record	Teachers communicate incident reports immediately.	As needed
Human Resources	Assist director in mentoring new employees.	Create a culture of mentorship	New teachers are assigned to an experienced teacher for mentorship.	As needed
Customer Service and Retention	• Notify the director of a family's disenrollment. • Write incident reports.		Teachers communicate disenrollment or incident reports immediately.	Weekly basis or as needed

	Work with families to help children progress toward educational and behavioral goals.	Parent-teacher conference	Teachers conduct parent-teacher conferences to communicate assessment data and plans for helping children reach educational and behavioral goals.	Every quarter

Step 7: Develop and Assess Your Team

Successful child-care centers share the same vision of quality, quantify results, and reward employees based on those results. Directors need to track to evaluate whether their actions are driving the desired outcomes.

The keys to quality are consistency in following processes and monitoring results to create accountability. The best way to monitor results is to use the framework of the dashboard during your weekly meetings. Measures without meetings are useless. This is the opportunity to ask your lead teachers specific questions related to your goals and action steps, such as, "What are you doing about this parent response?" and "What could you do to avoid this situation next time?"

Weekly Meeting Agenda with Lead Teachers

	TACTICAL GOALS	ACTUAL RESULTS
Operations		
Health and Safety		
Curriculum		
Licensing		
Human Resources		
Customer Service and Retention		

You can create and design the best program in the world, but if you are not able to recruit and retain the best executors of the vision, you will not fulfill the mission. There is an arsenal of ways in the industry to measure teacher performance. These tools can assist you in creating individualized learning plans.

Step 8: Reward Dedication and Achievement

Once you establish a framework to track progress, you are making each staff member accountable for her performance and can reward the behaviors you want to promote as best practice. For example, if you are trying to find teachers with the best classroom management practices, you can create a reward program around that skill and use the teacher to mentor others.

Step 9: Offer a Positive Exit When Needed

Terminating a staff member's employment is also part of the employee experience and is an event that might have legal and marketing repercussions. As a best practice, include in your staff handbook your termination procedures; confidentiality agreements; a noncompete agreement; and a nondisparagement agreement stating that the employee won't say anything negative about the company, its services, or leaders in any form of communication.

By using a consistent and fair process, you will reduce your liability. When a member of your management team notices underperformance, that person should start documenting the details. Discuss with your management team the expectations of the process, such as avoiding emotional language. Discuss the issue with the employee, and have someone other than the manager, such as the director, in the meeting. Give the employee time to improve. If the employee does not improve, then termination of employment is warranted.

| CONCLUSION |

We have the privilege of spending time with the best of humanity: young children. It is our duty to create learning environments that promote kindness, compassion, a joy for learning, and respect for each other.

Building a people-centered culture around accountability, expectations, and a strong mission is the best strategy for leading the child-care organizations of the future. This involves designing experiences to better the lives of early childhood professionals and creating systems to build a culture of accountability across your organization.

As leaders, the process is rooted in the way we view, advocate for, respect, and treat purpose-driven professionals in our industry and in a personal commitment to improve the environment and conditions to create a stable workforce for young children during the most critical years of brain development. As a manager, the systems and processes you create will provide the framework, expectations, and culture for the rest of your organization.

Self-help author Wayne Dyer once said, "See the light in others, and treat them as if that is all you see." If you expect only the best in others, your high performers will stay around and your low performers will feel so uncomfortable that they will not want to be part of your team.

Are you ready to lead?

REFERENCES AND RECOMMENDED READING

Abel, Michael, Teri Talan, and Marina Magid. 2018. *Closing the Leadership Gap: 2018 Status Report on Early Childhood Program Leadership in the United States.* Wheeling, IL: McCormick Center for Early Childhood Leadership.

Allvin, Rhian Evans, and Lauren Hogan. 2020. "There's No Going Back: Child Care after COVID-19." National Association for the Education of Young Children. https://www.naeyc.org/resources/blog/theres-no-going-back-child-care-after-covid-19

Andersen, Erika. 2012. "Are Leaders Born or Made?" *Forbes*, November 21. https://www.forbes.com/sites/erikaandersen/2012/11/21/are-leaders-born-or-made/#7ccf76be48d5

Ansel, Bridget. 2016. "Is the Cost of Childcare Driving Women Out of the U.S. Workforce?" Washington Center for Equitable Growth. https://equitablegrowth.org/is-the-cost-of-childcare-driving-women-out-of-the-u-s-workforce/

Betterteam. n.d. *New Hire Checklist.* Betterteam. https://www.betterteam.com/downloads/new-hire-checklist-download-20170907.pdf

Betterteam. 2020. "19 Recruitment Strategy Mistakes." Betterteam. https://www.betterteam.com/recruiting-strategies

Bishop-Josef, Sandra, et al. 2019. *Want to Grow the Economy? Fix the Child Care Crisis.* Washington, DC: Council for Strong America. https://www.americanprogress.org/issues/early-childhood/reports/2019/03/28/467488/child-care-crisis-keeping-women-workforce/#fn-467488-8

Brandon, Richard, et al. 2013. *Number and Characteristics of Early Care and Education (ECE) Teachers and Caregivers: Initial Findings from the National Survey of Early Care and Education (NSECE).* OPRE Report #2013-38. Washington, DC: Office of Planning, Research and Evaluation, Administration for Children and Families, US Department of Health and Human Services. https://www.acf.hhs.gov/sites/default/files/opre/nsece_wf_brief_102913_0.pdf

Bureau of Labor Statistics. 2019. "Occupational Outlook Handbook, Childcare Workers." US Department of Labor. https://www.bls.gov/ooh/personal-care-and-service/childcare-workers.htm

Carter, Margie, and Deb Curtis. 2009. *The Visionary Director: A Handbook for Dreaming, Organizing, and Improvising in Your Center.* 2nd ed. St. Paul, MN: Redleaf.

Center for the Study of Child Care Employment. 2018. "4 Early Childhood Workforce Policies." *Early Childhood Workforce Index 2018.* Berkeley, CA: Center for the Study of Child Care Employment, Institute for Research on Labor and Employment, University of California, Berkeley. https://cscce.berkeley.edu/files/2018/06/4-ECE-Policies.pdf

Center on the Developing Child. 2020. "Brain Architecture." Center on the Developing Child, Harvard University. https://developingchild.harvard.edu/science/key-concepts/brain-architecture/

Chertoff, Emily. 2013. "Reggio Emilia: From Postwar Italy to NYC's Toniest Preschools." *The Atlantic.* https://www.theatlantic.com/national/archive/2013/01/reggio-emilia-from-postwar-italy-to-nycs-toniest-preschools/267204/

Colker, Laura. 2008. "Twelve Characteristics of Effective Early Childhood Teachers." *Young Children* 63(2): 68–73.

Colker, Laura, and Derry Koralek. 2018. *High-Quality Early Childhood Programs: The What, Why, and How.* St. Paul, MN: Redleaf.

Darwin, Charles. 1859. *On the Origin of Species.* London, UK: John Murray.

Davidai, Shai, Sebastian Deri, and Thomas Gilovich. 2020. "There Must Be More to Life Than This: The Impact of Highly Accessible Exemplars on Self-

Evaluation and Discontent." *Self and Identity*. https://doi.org/10.1080/15298868.2020.1779121

Eckerson, Wayne. 2006. *Performance Dashboards: Measuring, Monitoring, and Managing Your Business*. Hoboken, NJ: John Wiley and Sons.

Frank, Robert H. 2016. "The Incalculable Value of Finding a Job You Love." *The New York Times*, July 24. https://www.nytimes.com/2016/07/24/upshot/first-rule-of-the-job-hunt-find-something-you-love-to-do.html

Gallup. n.d. "Engage Your Employees to See High Performance and Innovation." Gallup. https://www.gallup.com/workplace/229424/employee-engagement.aspx

Gallup. 2015. *State of the American Manager: Analytics and Advice for Leaders*. Washington, DC: Gallup.

Glassdoor. 2016. "Essential HR and Recruiting Stats for 2016." Glassdoor for Employers. https://www.glassdoor.com/employers/blog/essential-hr-recruiting-stats-2016/

Glassdoor. 2018. "Building an Employer Brand from Scratch." Glassdoor for Employers. https://www.glassdoor.com/employers/blog/how-to-create-an-employer-brand-from-scratch/

Goleman, Daniel. 2004. "What Makes a Leader?" *Harvard Business Review*. https://hbr.org/2004/01/what-makes-a-leader

Griffith, Erin. 2020. "Airbnb Was Like a Family, Until the Layoffs Started." *The New York Times*, July 29. https://www.nytimes.com/2020/07/17/technology/airbnb-coronavirus-layoffs-.html

Halpin, John, Karl Agne, and Margie Omero. 2018. *Affordable Child Care and Early Learning for All Families: A National Public Opinion Study*. Washington, DC: Center for American Progress. https://cdn.americanprogress.org/content/uploads/2018/09/12074422/ChildCarePolling-report.pdf

Hart, Meredith. 2019. "12 Examples of Positioning Statements and How to Craft Your Own." HubSpot. https://blog.hubspot.com/sales/positioning-statement

Haughey, Duncan. 2014. "A Brief History of SMART Goals." Project Smart. https://www.projectsmart.co.uk/brief-history-of-smart-goals.php

HiMama. 2019. *The 2019 Child Care Benchmark Report: Statistics and Industry Trends.* https://blog.himama.com/benchmark-2019/

Hunt, James M., and Joseph R. Weintraub. 2017. *The Coaching Manager: Developing Top Talent in Business.* 3rd ed. Thousand Oaks, CA: SAGE.

Kaplan, Robert, and David P. Norton. 1992. "The Balanced Scorecard—Measures that Drive Performance." *Harvard Business Review.* https://hbr.org/1992/01/the-balanced-scorecard-measures-that-drive-performance-2

Kurzweil, Ray. 2000. *The Age of Spiritual Machines: When Computers Exceed Human Intelligence.* New York: Penguin.

Laurano, Madeline. 2013. *Onboarding 2013: A New Look at New Hires.* Aberdeen Group. https://deliberatepractice.com.au/wp-content/uploads/2013/04/Onboarding-2013.pdf

Maurer, Roy. 2015. "Onboarding Key to Retaining, Engaging Talent." Society for Human Resource Management. https://www.shrm.org/resourcesandtools/hr-topics/talent-acquisition/pages/onboarding-key-retaining-engaging-talent.aspx#:~:text=%E2%80%9CUnfortunately%2C%20only%2015%20percent%20of,huge%20impact%20on%20that%20choice

McCormick Center for Early Childhood Leadership. 2010. "A Window on Early Childhood Administrative Practices." Executive summary. Wheeling, IL: McCormick Center for Early Childhood Leadership Publications, National Louis University. https://digitalcommons.nl.edu/cgi/viewcontent.cgi?article=1021&context=mccormickcenter-pubs

MindTools. n.d. "SMART Goals: How to Make Your Goals Achievable." MindTools. https://www.mindtools.com/pages/article/smart-goals.htm

Morgan, Jacob. 2017. *The Employee Experience Advantage: How to Win the War for Talent by Giving Employees the Workspaces They Want, the Tools They Need, and a Culture They Can Celebrate.* Hoboken, NJ: John Wiley and Sons.

Morgan, Jacob. 2017. "The War for Talent: It's Real and Here's Why It's Happening." Inc. https://www.inc.com/jacob-morgan/the-war-for-talent-its-real-heres-why-its-happening.html

Murphy, Mark. 2016. *Hiring for Attitude: A Revolutionary Approach to Recruiting and Selecting People with Both Tremendous Skills and Superb Attitude.* New York: McGraw-Hill.

National Association for the Education of Young Children. n.d. "Accreditation Process for Early Learning Programs." NAEYC. https://www.naeyc.org/accreditation/early-learning/process#Enroll

National Scientific Council on the Developing Child. 2004. "Young Children Develop in an Environment of Relationships." Working Paper 1. Center on the Developing Child, Harvard University. http://developingchild.harvard.edu/wp-content/uploads/2004/04/Young-Children-Develop-in-an-Environment-of-Relationships.pdf

New Age Leadership. n.d. "360 Degree Feedback." New Age Leadership. https://newageleadership.com/360-degree-feedback/

Next Generation. n.d. "The Difference between Leadership and Management." Next Generation. https://www.nextgeneration.ie/blog/2018/03/the-difference-between-leadership-and-management#:~:text=Leadership%20is%20about%20getting%20people,are%20happening%20as%20they%20should

Office of Child Care. 2015. "Trends in Child Care Center Licensing Regulations and Policies for 2014." Washington, DC: US Department of Health and Human Services. https://childcareta.acf.hhs.gov/resource/research-brief-1-trends-child-care-center-licensing-regulations-and-policies-2014

Oxford University Press. 2020. "Search Engine Optimization." Oxford Languages. https://languages.oup.com/google-dictionary-en/

Pianta, Robert, and Megan Stuhlman. 2004. "Teacher-Child Relationships and Children's Success in the First Years of School." *School Psychology Review* 33(3): 444–458. http://pages.erau.edu/~andrewsa/Project_2/Christian_John/DuneProject/Teaching.pdf

QRIS National Learning Network. 2017. "Current Status of QRIS in States: January 2017." Boston, MA: BUILD Initiative. http://qrisnetwork.org/sites/all/files/maps/QRISMap_0.pdf

Richards, Tressa S. n.d. "Social Media Recruitment Strategies that Work." Rally. https://rallyrecruitmentmarketing.com/2019/10/social-media-recruitment-strategies/

Ritchhart, Ron. 2015. *Creating Cultures of Thinking: The 8 Forces We Must Master to Truly Transform Our Schools.* San Francisco: Jossey-Bass.

Robison, Jennifer. 2008. "Turning Around Employee Turnover." Gallup. https://news.gallup.com/businessjournal/106912/turning-around-your-turnover-problem.aspx

Russell, Elizabeth M., Sue W. Williams, and Cheryl Gleason-Gomez. 2010. "Teachers' Perceptions of Administrative Support and Antecedents of Turnover." *Journal of Research in Childhood Education* 24(3): 195–208.

Salesforce. 2020. "Create Organizational Alignment through the V2MOM." Trailhead. https://trailhead.salesforce.com/en/content/learn/modules/manage_the_sfdc_organizational_alignment_v2mom/msfw_oav2m_creating_org_alignment_v2mom

Schochet, Leila. 2019. "The Child Care Crisis Is Keeping Women Out of the Workforce." Center for American Progress. https://www.americanprogress.org/issues/early-childhood/reports/2019/03/28/467488/child-care-crisis-keeping-women-workforce/#fn-467488-8

Siebert, Terry. 2017. "The 'Innerview': A Tool for Employee Engagement." *InBusiness Madison.* https://www.ibmadison.com/the-innerview-a-tool-for-employee-engagement/

Society for Human Resource Management. 2020. "Managing the Employee Onboarding and Assimilation Process." Society for Human Resource Management. https://shrm.org/resourcesandtools/tools-and-samples/toolkits/pages/onboardingandassimilationprocess.aspx?_ga=2.173755427.1627870858.1598985185-132499595.1598985185

Sostrin, Jesse. 2017. "To Be a Great Leader, You Have to Learn How to Delegate Well." *Harvard Business Review.* https://hbr.org/2017/10/to-be-a-great-leader-you-have-to-learn-how-to-delegate-well

Stevens, Katharine. 2017. *Workforce of Today, Workforce of Tomorrow: The Business Case for High-Quality Childcare.* Washington, DC: US Chamber of Commerce Foundation.

Strock, James. 2018. *Serve to Lead: 21st Century Leaders Manual.* 2nd ed. Scotts Valley, CA: CreateSpace.

Surr, John. 2004. "Who's Accredited? What and How the States Are Doing on Best Practices in Child Care." *Child Care Information Exchange* 156(2): 14–22. https://www.childcareexchange.com/library/5015614.pdf

Thurston, Philip. 1986. "When Partners Fall Out." *Harvard Business Review.* https://hbr.org/1986/11/when-partners-fall-out

Toister, Jeff. 2017. *The Service Culture Handbook: A Step-by-Step Guide to Getting Your Employees Obsessed with Customer Service.* San Diego, CA: Toister Performance Solutions.

Torquati, Julia, Helen Raikes, and Catherine Huddleston-Casas. 2007. "Teacher Education, Motivation, Compensation, Workplace Support, and Links to Quality of Center-Based Child Care and Teachers' Intention to Stay in the Early Childhood Profession." *Early Childhood Research Quarterly* 22(2): 261–275.

University of Pittsburgh Office of Human Resources. n.d. *Job Description Writing Guide.* https://www.hr.pitt.edu/sites/default/files/JobDescriptionWritingGuide.pdf

US Department of Health and Human Services. 2015. *Research Brief #1: Trends in Child Care Center Licensing Regulations and Policies for 2014.* Washington, DC: Administration for Children and Families, Office of Child Care.

Vander Ark, Thomas. 2017. "The Future of Skills: Employment in 2030." Getting Smart. https://www.gettingsmart.com/2017/09/the-future-of-skills-employment-in-2030/#:~:text=Our%20research%20definitively%20shows%20that,to%20boost%20demand%20for%20jobs

Whitebook, Marcy, et al. 2018. *Early Childhood Workforce Index—2018*. Berkeley, CA: Center for the Study of Child Care Employment, University of California, Berkeley. http://cscce.berkeley.edu/topic/early-childhood-workforce-index/2018/

Wolfe, Ira S. 2017. *Recruiting in the Age of Googlization: When the Shift Hits Your Plan*. Melbourne, FL: Motivational Press.

Workman, Simon, and Rebecca Ullrich. 2017. "Quality 101: Identifying the Core Components of a High-Quality Early Childhood Program." Center for American Progress. https://www.americanprogress.org/issues/early-childhood/reports/2017/02/13/414939/quality-101-identifying-the-core-components-of-a-high-quality-early-childhood-program/

Yonahara, Cathleen, and Mark Schickman. 2012. "5 Critical Components Every Job Description Must Contain." HR Daily Advisor. https://hrdailyadvisor.blr.com/2012/02/15/5-critical-components-every-job-description-must-contain/

Zojceska, Anja. 2018. "HR Metrics: How and Why to Calculate Employee Turnover Rate." TalentLyft. https://www.talentlyft.com/en/blog/article/242/hr-metrics-how-and-why-to-calculate-employee-turnover-rate

INDEX

CARROLL COUNTY
OCT 2021
PUBLIC LIBRARY

WITHDRAWN FROM LIBRARY